How Our Minds *Really* Work

It Ain't Pretty

A Brief Adventure Into

The Evolved Structures In

The Catacombs Of Our Mind

M. R. Lauer

The Pinnacle Quest series:

Technical Series

Pinnacle Questions

Pinnacle Reasoning

Ultrareasoning: Principles and Practices of Faceted Model-Oriented Reasoning

The Structure of Truth

General Problem Theory: A Framework for Problem Solving In The Unknown

Popular Series

How Our Minds Really Work: It Ain't Pretty

Super Stupid: Why The Educated Elite Are So Wrong So Often About So Many Things

Cover image © 2018 - Rube Goldberg Inc.

2

Neither agree,

nor disagree;

explore

and

discover.

Contents

List of Figures

Preface

This is a conversational flyover of the material presented in full technical detail in a series of volumes: *Ultrareasoning, Structure of Truth,* and *General Problem Theory.* The purpose of this small book is to make the very difficult material from those textbooks accessible to everyone who is curious about why the mind sometimes works in such weird ways.

This will be a brief journey into parts of your mind that you never knew existed, but will likely immediately recognize as soon as they are pointed out. If you relax and enjoy the trip, instead of sweating the details, you'll find it easier to get a good idea of the big concepts that explain how the structure of our mind evolved into what it is today. Knowing that, you'll be able to understand why the mind works the way it does.

What you do with this new knowledge is up to you,

but buckle up, because I promise you, this is going to be quite a surprising journey.

Part I

Ideas In The Toolkit

Chapter 1

In The Beginning

Let me tell you a story about your mind, it begins with a fact that you should already know: your mind doesn't work the way you think it does, not even close. It regularly doesn't work the way you expect it to, not when you make decisions, not when you deal with feelings or moral issues, and not when you make plans for the future. The evidence for this? Your daily experience with surprise, frustration, and disappointment when things don't work out the way you expected them to.

Ask yourself, why is disappointment with your fellow humans a weekly, if not daily or hourly, experience? We're human, they're human, we're all built of the same stuff, so why are we so often startled and dismayed by their perfectly predictable words and actions? Only one reason

I can think of: we barely have a clue about how the mind works, whether it's the one in our head or theirs.

Who am I to talk about this? Some kind of expert who knows how to live better than you do? Hardly. No, I'm just the guy who crawled out from under your car to give you the bad news about what's kind of broken and what's really broken under there.

And no, I'm not some kind of idiot intellectual who wants to sell you an ideology, or tell you what to think. No, after you've read this story about the inner workings of your mind, you'll find that I haven't sold you a new ideology, religion, or even a new fad diet.

Think of me as a toolmaker, I make the wrenches, presses, cutting, and measuring tools for the mind. What you do with them is up to you, entirely up to you. I can explain that a particular wrench set is of high quality and what it can be used for, but you're on your own when the time comes to fix or customize your car or your mind.

I might even draw your attention to what I think is a really interesting tool, even though I might have no idea what you could or would ever want to do with it. With a lot of this stuff, I'm more interested in seeing how people will use it in new ways that I never anticipated. Tools only achieve their full potential in the hands of dedicated and inventive craftsmen, not when they are just sitting in their case, and all I do is build the tools and put them in boxes on the shelf. The rest is up to you.

Now, don't get me wrong, I'm good, *really* good at what I do. I mean incredibly good, but whether that should mean anything to you is for you to figure out. I just make the tools — and by tools, I mean models, concepts, and theoretical frameworks — I'm not the guy who uses them, not the mechanic or the carpenter. But, being a toolmaker is a good, honest trade.

Why should you be interested in the tools I've created? Well, you've got this brain inside of your head that is capable of some pretty amazing stuff, but almost everything you think you know about it, or about how to make it do what you want it to do, is wrong. Now, this doesn't mean I want to, or could, lead you to the light. It may be hard to believe, but I really don't care what you think, believe, or like. I'm not even saying that learning how your mind actually works will necessarily change any of your ideas, or the way you live your life, or even that it should. All I know is that it will give you some completely new ways of seeing things. What you do, or don't do, with that knowledge is entirely up to you.

We'll start by introducing a bunch of important concepts in this chapter about the structure of our mind. These are ideas you will need to know in order to understand how your brain really works. Once you get an overview of the ideas involved, you should see that it will all start to make sense, and that it's not that much of a stretch to comprehend. Understanding how reasoning naturally evolves in all animals will make it much easier for you to understand how and why you think, see, and act the way you do in your own life.

Ideas And Models

The tools I will be telling you about, and showing you how to use, are `models`. Now, ideas and models are very different things, they are not just synonyms for each other. Any notion floating around in your mind can be considered an idea, but an idea can become a model only if you strip away all of your personal values and experiences related to it, and rephrase it in a formal language.

We think in *ideas*, bits of thought that are personal and subjective because they really only make sense when they are embedded in our own specific experiences and values. We can try to communicate ideas to each other using words and images, but they won't be fully understood, because the listener has to wrap them in their own experiences and values in order to make the ideas meaningful and relatable in their own life. The problem is that doing that significantly changes the ideas from what they meant to the speaker into what they now mean to the listener.

The only effective way to fully communicate an idea is to express it in a formal language that excludes personal experiences and values so that it can be independently understood and tested by any other competent observer, that is, to make it into a `model`. If the other person gets the same result with their test, then the statement can be considered verified, although not necessarily completely, forever, or in all contexts.

In other words, an idea is invisibly wrapped in your own feelings, values, and experiences, and hence is subjective and incommunicable, while a model is unambiguously defined in formal terms without your feelings or values included, and it can be tested in external reality without reference to your own opinion of it.

You really have to grasp this difference between ideas and models if you want to understand any of the concepts we are going to discuss, since they are all models, not just ideas. Periodically throughout this book, we will occasionally refer to models as ideas and ideas as models when it helps the conversation flow easier, but as long as you are clear that models can be tested, while ideas can only be agreed or disagreed with, you'll be okay.

The Beginning

Our story begins with how it came to be that, even though we think with our mind all day, every day, somehow we do this without ever clearly understanding how it really works, even when we're trying hard to figure it out. This inability to see directly into our mind is a showstopping problem that stymies us right at the starting gate in the struggle to figure out how our minds work. Except for that, we likely would all be able to figure out the rest of the story by ourselves.

But, the sad fact is the first thing about our mind you don't understand is that it is structurally incapable of studying itself. Whoops. You gotta admit that presents us with a little problem. This structural barrier to self-knowledge is called the `purblind defect`, the inability of the mind to peer inside of itself and see its constituent parts. `Purblind` means *really* blind, and the purblind defect describes the fact that we can only see our mind from the very specific and biased point of view of our feelings and our words, not from a higher perspective from which we could see everything.

Our ideas are built from words and expressed in words. But words and feelings are as far from the center of our mind as the earth is from the center of our solar system. And, remember, it took people thousands of years to figure out that the earth wasn't actually the center of the entire universe. So, perhaps we shouldn't be too surprised that we're only now beginning to figure out that our rational consciousness is nowhere near the center of our mind.

The reality is that, instead of being able to look at our mind from a perspective that would give us a good overview of everything, we are actually caught in a little cave in a deep gully on the downside of a far hill, and the view we have of all things mental is inherently biased towards feelings and word ideas, and consequently is hopelessly muddled. The problem is that trying to see our mind from the perspective of word ideas, instead of *evolved structures*, is a fatal mistake. It locks us into the untenable notion that words naturally describe reality as it really is, when actually all they do is just let us express our inner feelings in a way that makes it possible for us to live and work in groups (sure, words do more than that, but just chew on this for a while, and we'll get to the rest of it in the next few chapters).

Be honest, how often have you contextualized your feelings and ideas in a structure-based model of the mind? Most assuredly never, even though you know that humans start out as just a collection of all sorts of different little structures that are specified by our genetic blueprint. Given that, shouldn't our first choice for understanding our mind have been a structural model? Of course it should have, but that's not the way we think, is it?

True, not everything is structure, we do get more complicated as we add experience to our makeup, but that's just the salt in the stew. The meat and potatoes is all inherited, genetically defined structures and the functionality associated with them.

Why our species evolved mentally over time, while other species remained more or less unchanged, is not our problem to solve here. But, the laboratory of life gives us a living evolutionary record in the form of various animals who remain at different, lower intellect levels than us. What may be a surprise is that these levels are all still active in our own, evolved working mind today.

It should not be a surprise that cognitive ability evolved over a long period of time, developing from the simple to the complex, and that the highest cognitive powers didn't just suddenly drop from the sky into our mind one day.

Just by looking at the spectrum of creatures from insects and amoebas to birds, rodents, and primates, we can see innumerable examples that demonstrate that the higher intellect developed only gradually, one level, at a time.

The structure-based model that we will be using to explore our mind gives us an entirely different, and much more powerful way to understand why the mind works the way it does. This new framework, this model, will prove to be immensely more productive and useful than the traditional view of our mind as an uneasy mix of emotional feelings and rational thoughts. The structural approach will enable us to see that the mind evolved from the more primitive to its current state in successive layers, and that humans weren't just suddenly endowed with a rational, modern mind infused with self-awareness all at once, but that we share much of our mental equipment with most of the animal kingdom.

Keep in mind that evolution does not often replace a working layer, instead it enhances, edits, or elaborates it, thus keeping much or all of the previous functionality in place as a working base for the newer developments.

Of interest to us is the grouping of a set of mutations that produces a new species periodically over time. It is this grouping and periodic replacement that leads to the phenomenon of layers in our cognitive apparatus, our mind. The earliest evolutionary layer will have a certain set of abilities, and then a later layer will add new abilities and modifications, and so on, without disrupting the earlier layer. We know this to be so because the evidence is all around us.

The purblind defect makes it difficult to impossible for us to see these layered, evolved structures that accumulated through the ages. However, unlike in an archaeological dig where everything is lifeless, each of these layers is still functioning in us, still contributing to, and still influencing our essential thought processes. Due to the defect, instead of seeing the layers that, if we understand evolution at all, we know have to be there, what we see is a confederated emotional/rational mechanism that we mistake for a modern, rational mind that somehow has the power to show us reality in precise and complete detail.

Certainly, our mind is made up of layers of older, more primitive *but still functioning* minds topped off by a layer that thinks and communicates in words. This means that the very earliest part of our mind that evaluates perceptions and decides to approach, retreat, or ignore something, well, it's still there, and it is still working every waking minute of every day pretty much the same way that it works in the squirrel brain. It produces output that the other parts of our brain may reprocess, but the higher layers interpret the output from the lower layers in their own more advanced idiom, and completely miss the true primitive nature of it. Higher layers of our mind think that what they are getting from the lower levels is a true picture of reality, instead of the fairly crude evaluation of perception that it actually is.

While we are aware of the difference between thoughts and feelings, we are not very clear about the distinction between the different types of thoughts that the several levels of our mind can think. Of course, the purblind defect makes it impossible for us to see this directly, so this is why we need *tools* in the form of models and theories (this is where I come in) that allow us to indirectly 'see' the different structural parts of our mind.

Because our awareness, our consciousness, is centered in our ability to formulate and express feelings and ideas with words, we unconsciously assume that the purpose of our mind is to reason about, and understand, both ideas and reality, because that's what our word-mind thinks it does. This skewed notion couldn't be any more wrong. Thinking dispassionately and rationally about reality is more of a mirage than a true function, more of an artifact of the structures on which verbal thought is based, than any kind of accurate description of what our mind actually does.

No, the function of our cognitive abilities, our cognition system, is not, in fact, *knowledge*, but **evaluation.** That's a big difference, a HUGE difference. The function of our brain is most emphatically *not* to be able to see, know, and understand externalities, i.e., things out there. Rather, it is to allow us to process sensory input into an action response that might help us to survive and thrive in the here and now.

Think about this for a moment: in order for animals to survive, their choices for when and how to move, must, on average, help them to survive long enough to procreate, or the species would go extinct. The core question of voluntary motion is: should I approach, retreat from, or ignore the thing I perceive? The question, *what is that thing?* is of no concern or interest. What is of interest to us are the attributes of the thing: is it big, powerful, moving towards us, does it have carnivorous jaws, and so on. These attributes are important and go into our evaluation, but what that thing is, in and of itself, has no meaning to our basic, mortality-focused intellect. Nor should it. In reality, it is much less important for us to understand what a thing is, than it is to move *as if* we do. We can get away with mistaking a mouse for an elephant as long as we move in such as way as to survive the encounter with minimal cost and some benefit.

Volitionally mobile creatures (animals) embody the proposition that **a movement solution exists for every problem**, and this means that it is more important to move quickly enough in a direction that is, on average, survivable, in order to preserve our reproductive potential, than it is to know anything about whatever that thing out there actually is. As long as we survive, then whether we lose opportunities or over estimate risks is just a negligible detail for which we automatically compensate by always being on the hunt, since **seek** is our default waking action.

Our cognitive system exists to evaluate signals that come from our internal and external senses so that we can answer the approach-retreat-ignore question every waking moment of every day. We all know about the five external senses: sight, hearing, smell, touch, and taste, but few seem to be aware of the internal senses, which are at least equally important. There are many more internal senses than external senses, including: a sense of thirst, hunger, fatigue, strength, vitality, sexual attraction, ambition, and expectation, and so on.

The input of the internal senses is the difference between *evaluation* of other and *reacting* to other. Our assessment of *other* is based primarily on input from the external senses, but our calculation of an appropriate *reaction* requires balancing our sense of our own resources and needs, which we get from our internal senses, with our estimation of threat and opportunity we get from the external ones.

There is a structure in our mind called the `action module` that performs the work of combining evaluations of the internal and external senses to produce an action command that is sent to the body to carry out. It is remarkable how little the `action module` has changed since animal life first appeared. The purblind defect makes us think that it is our thoughts and feelings that drive our actions, and indirectly they do, but they do this only after our most complex thoughts and impassioned feelings are reduced to the threat/opportunity/unimportant form that the `action module` processes into an action command that triggers movement.

Approach/retreat/ignore (qualified with some level of urgency) is the command sent to the body once the mind evaluates input. The `action module` is a primordial structure we share with virtually (or all) animals on the tree of life; it is the structure that takes in the good/bad/ indifferent evaluation and converts that to an approach/ retreat/ignore command that the body can implement as an action. An indication of how primitive the action module is can be seen when you understand that the **retreat fast** command doesn't have to change from species to species, because birds, fish, and quadrupeds can implement the action in completely different ways in their own bodily idiom without requiring any changes to the action command language itself.

This tripolar anti-self, pro-self, non-self response paradigm is the basis of all of our cognitive ability, the basis of all of our emotions, the basis of all of our behavior. When we program simulations of real human behavior, this tripolar nature of evaluation is captured in a data structure we call the **evacule**, the *atom of evaluation*, the fundamental unit of all of our thoughts and feelings, both in life and in the simulation.

Evacule [a, p, n] Attributes:

   a, anti-self: threat

   p, pro-self: opportunity

   n, non-self: nullity

The **evacule** is represented by an array structure that

has three elements: the anti-self or hate part, the pro-self or love part, and the non-self or indifferent part. Each part has a value between minimum (zero) and maximum. If we say that there are 10 possible values in the range, that means that the evacule can record $10^3 = 1,000$ different emotional responses.

I don't know about you, but I've never met anyone, or read anything, that suggests that humans have that many significantly different emotions. However, if we cut that down to 5 possible values in the range, then that would give us $5^3 = 125$ different emotional responses, and that might be just enough or a little light, so let's say that the value for maximum is somewhere between 5 and 10, giving us somewhere between 125 and 1,000 different emotions in our emotional repertoire.[1]

The power of the evacule is that it shows how simply our emotional responses can be encoded genetically or programmatically, and it gives us a workable model that shows how our emotions, our self-interest, and our decision-making ability all come together in one tiny little model that we can use to clarify some messy thinking, and to dispel confusion.

---

[1]Which number we choose doesn't really matter, since it's just a parameter in our model that we can adjust whenever we feel the need.

At the most basic level, that's it, that's what organic cognition is all about, because we embody the proposition that **movement solutions exist to all mortality problems**. In the end, all of our thinking *has* to boil down to an approach/retreat/ignore choice that can be sent to our body to initiate action.

What you need to understand is that the traditional bipole view of values, such as love/hate, good/bad, true/false, right/wrong, is oversimplified and misleading. The evacule encodes three values instead of two: anti-self, pro-self, *and* non-self. This encompasses: good, bad, *and* unimportant; true/false/*and* don't care; love/hate/*and* indifferent. Not valuing something enough to give it attention, not caring about it, being alienated from it, or being bored by it, is as much a first order emotion as are love and hate. It is impossible to understand emotion without first understanding that the emotional spectrum is a tripolar value system. The complexity of our emotional repertoire comes from the numerous mixtures of the three components combined together in all of the different permutations possible.[2]

It's not a coincidence that love/hate/indifference maps directly to approach/retreat/ignore, because they are two

---

[2]See *The Structure Of Truth.*

sides of the same coin, they are the evaluation and the re-action sides of processing sensory input from a self-interested perspective. Labeling this perceptual-reaction system as self-interest-based is not to denigrate it, because as mortal creatures, we, both as individuals and as species represen-tatives, can only survive to perpetuate our species if we tend to respond to our world in a self-preferential way.

While the `action module` has remained basically un-changed, the rest of our mind has evolved over time by adding new layers of functionality, most of which are shared, at least partially, with many other species. Only the query engine[3] seems to be unique to humans, and very few hu-mans are even aware of its existence, or what it can do, let alone how to use it.[4]

---

[3]See below.

[4]See *General Problem Theory* for a deep treatment of the nature and power of **L3** **after** you have read *Super Stupid* or *Ultrareasoning*.

Chapter 2

Levels

This isn't complicated: the mind evolved in layers, from the simplest to the most complex. The earlier layers don't know about the later ones, but the later ones do know how to access the earlier ones. How could it be otherwise?

The division of labor between the layers is the most obvious and natural arrangement that you could imagine:

- the first layer, L0, gives us the ability to react to the present;
- the second layer, L1, gives us the ability to remember and to learn from experience, the past;
- the third layer, L2, gives us the ability to plan and execute tasks step by step, and to anticipate the future;
- the fourth layer, L3, enables us to query the un-

known.

See? Simple:

- L0: present

- L1: past

- L2: future

- L3: unknown

Of course, these layers are just layers in the model that we are using to understand our mind. They are not even necessarily the best or only set of layers we could imagine, nor do they necessarily map to specific structures in the physical mind. What they are supposed to do — and what they succeed in doing very well — is to simulate and predict observable behaviors, not only in humans, but in all animals that we care to observe. The result is that we can create simulations that behave the same way that humans and animals do, and this is why this model is a useful tool that we can use to probe our own mind and behavior.

Since we can't see inside of ourself, when we want to try to figure out how certain things — like opinions, for example — work, we can program them up in the model and test until we can replicate observed behavior, then we can see which behaviors came from which levels of intellect.

The model of the evolutionary stages that exist in our

mind has these four layers, that we call levels of intellect, with the following functionality:

L0: Level zero gives us the ability to approach opportunity, retreat from threat, and ignore the inconsequential by recognizing different degrees of similarity between perceptions and inherited archetypes of good and bad.

L1: Level one gives us the ability to remember the results of our actions, thus giving us the ability to learn from experience.

L2: Level two gives us the ability to see and remember patterns in experience, to anticipate potential future events, and to use language to manage social relations.

L3: Level three gives us the ability to systematically explore the unknown.

Each of these four mental levels has functions that operate on the inherited structures in that level. Higher levels can convert lower level structures into their own more complex versions, and convert their structures to simpler, lower level ones, but lower levels cannot even know the higher levels exist.

The data structures in each level are:

L0: The `evacule` [anti-self, pro-self, non-self] structure

that provides the basis for evaluation, decision, belief, and emotion. The `mentacule` is an ordered array of evacules representing the various sensory inputs.

L1: The `result` object records the situation before an action, the action, and the situation after the action, as well as an evaluation of whether we are better or worse off from doing the action. The success of the action is calculated by comparing the before and after situations. The evaluation becomes the lesson we learned from the event.

L2: The `pattern` object allows us to match the current situation (a snapshot of current memory) to an appropriate response action, and then select from up to 7 or so optional paths we previously set up, which we can choose for our next step. Language is built upon the pattern object.

L3: The `query` object allows us to probe the unknown in a disciplined fashion.

We live and think in L2 because language is built on the pattern object. When we are looking to experience for guidance, we are in L1. When we are making decisions, dealing with beliefs, absolute truth, or when we are certain about anything, we are in L0.

The chapter on language will show that each level owns certain words by owning the concepts behind them. This distribution of concepts among the various levels makes thinking in language a tricky proposition since, just by using the wrong word in a given situation, we can fall through a trap door into an earlier, more primitive intellect that severely limits our ability to rationally consider all available options. For example, since logic is an L2 concept, we can use it to try to frame our argument, but should we, at any point, become *certain* that our logic is *absolutely* right, then just by doing that, we have abandoned our rational, logical mind and retreated into our primordial L0 intellect where certainty lives and rationality dies.

Chapter 3

Terms and Laws

I want to boil down the concepts we covered in the previous chapters to a few little nuggets that are easy to understand and remember. The goal is for you to have them at your fingertips so that, as we go deeper into the catacombs, you can always understand how we got there and how to get out again, without having to struggle to remember some term or connection.

Once you have these basic ideas sorted, you should find that you are surprised less and less often about how the mind is wired and how it works. Eventually, after you understand the underlying mechanisms, you will be able to easily understand why things happen as they do, even when they aren't to your liking.

First, here are a few definitions of the terms we are

using. Simple, clear definitions are easier to understand and remember.

DEFINITIONS

Model: a formalized, quantifiable, testable idea.

Idea: an informal notion, any notion that floats around in your mind.

Cognition: the process that begins with sensory perception, proceeds through evaluation and reasoning and ends up with an action solution.

Reasoning: the third step in the cognition process. It involves pattern recall, manipulation, and extension.

MODEL You create a model from an idea by stripping out personal and cultural values, and replacing them with numerical parameters so that you can write programs or formulas to test what happens when their values vary from least to most. Some other steps are necessary, but just keep in mind that a model is an impersonal, quantifiable idea with specific parameters that support a range of tests.

IDEA There is no such thing as a well-formed or badly formed idea. Ideas are just the basic unit of thought. They have links to our values, needs, expectations, and experiences, which is why it is hard to communicate important, personal ideas to other people. Since everyone else's value context is different than our own, when they try to take in our idea, it winds up meaning something different to them than it does to us because of how they hook it up to their values and memories.

COGNITION The whole process that starts with sensory input and ends with body action: perceive → identify → evaluate → remember → consider → plan → act.

REASONING Reasoning is just thinking, the remember → consider → plan part of cognition. Reasoning is what you are doing right now to try to make sense of what you are reading, for example. It's worth noting that normal reasoning is done on ideas using words, not models, because reasoning is usually informal and done in natural language, while models must be worked out in a formal language to be sound.

Seeing Within

If the purblind defect prevents us from looking into our own mind, then what are we going to be looking at throughout the rest of this book? We are going to be using models that will let us indirectly see things that we cannot see directly. This is not a new idea. For example, when physicists first began trying to probe the atom, Charles Wilson invented the cloud chamber that let them see the paths of invisible ionizing particles. Thus, they could study particles they could not see by causing them to leave visible trails.

The Universal Cognition Model is a large theoretical framework that allows us to combine the subjective and objective worlds together in a way that enables us to thoroughly test the full range of events that can occur in the subjective world by using formal models in the place of subjective ideas and personal anecdotes. We don't need to get down into the nitty gritty details of the UCM in order to use it, but we do have to understand a handful of its laws that describe how cognition works.

LAWS

There are six critical laws of the Universal Cognition Model. They are short, memorable, and profoundly useful. Discussions of each follow the list.

LAW 1: The mind cannot directly see inside of itself.

LAW 2: We think inside of our head on evolved structures.

LAW 3: Cognition is evaluation-based.

LAW 4: Evaluation is at least tripolar.

LAW 5: Perception is reductive.

LAW 6: Error exceeds content.

LAW 1: The mind cannot see inside itself

The purblind defect is real, and the only way we can even begin to work around it is to learn model-oriented reasoning. For now, just stop deluding yourself that you know how your mind is structured. Be open to a little rigorous tuition on the subject.

LAW 2: We think inside of our head on evolved structures

Seriously, how hard is it to understand that we think inside of our head? How can you argue with that? And, if we think inside of our head, which we surely do, then you have to ask, on *what* do we think? On structures, of course. After all, what else is inside of our head? And where do those structures come from? Do they just magically appear inside our head? No, of course not, we inherit them, they are specced out in our genetic blueprint.

And how did that blueprint come to be? Are we the first and only creature who can think at any level? Of course not, the ability to think has evolved slowly, over time, in all creatures who can move of their own free will.

Advanced life evolved from simpler life, advanced cognitive abilities evolved from simpler cognitive abilities, and our mind evolved from simpler minds.

How does evolutionary development work? Does it wipe the slate clean and start from scratch for each new species? No, it doesn't, our mind evolved from earlier hominid minds, which evolved from earlier primate minds, and so on. The earlier layers of the mind were not, for the most part, radically altered by the progress of evolution. The action module and the L0 level work exactly the same in us as they do in our dogs and cats, squirrels and hawks, deer and lions. Most importantly, the action module and L0 are still alert and active, and fully involved in every moment of every day of our life.

The mudball model of the mind is the notion that our mind is an integrated whole that flawlessly processes sensory input that we rationally examine to come up with a complete and correct understanding of reality. Even though this is a ridiculous model (we are calling it a model as a courtesy, but it really is just an unexamined idea that permeates intellectual circles), it is nevertheless the idea used by almost everyone, almost all the time.

Is it hard to realize that, as a consequence of long term evolution, we have accumulated several layers of intellect that, when taken together, collectively make up our ability to reason and to know? It shouldn't be. We think inside of our head on evolved, layered structures that can interact with older structures, but are unaware of newer structures.

It simply makes no sense to try to understand how our mind works without distributing functionality into successive layers. If your model of your mind is that it is a unitary rational mechanism, rather than a layered complex of specialized, simpler functions, then you are not modeling the human mind at all.

Yes, we think inside of our head on structures that evolved in layers over time, that much is clear and it seems so simple, yet, somehow, everyone seems to completely lose the plot on the very next step: thinking inside of our head means that we *perceive* inside our head, we *know* inside our head, we *feel* inside our head, and *the world we know is in a model inside our head.*

- We perceive inside of our head. Our external senses pick up signals from the outside world, but the signals mean nothing until they are decoded (or encoded, depending on how you look at it) inside of our head. The tree we see is actually inside our head. This does not mean that there is no tree outside of us, or that our internal idea of it has nothing to do with the external thing, just that whatever we see of the tree is inside of our head because, even though light rays are bouncing off the real tree into our eyes, we have to make sense of that information inside of our head before we can know anything. Those of us still alive today can bet that our inner picture of the tree roughly matches the external tree in its most important attributes, else we would have blindly stumbled into death's grip by now.

- We know inside of our head. We think we know there is a tree out there, and sometimes we can verify that it is out there, but how much of our idea of the tree matches the real tree? If you've ever been surprised that the tree you're trying to cut down is rotted out in the middle, you have experienced how dangerous it can be when your knowledge, your expectations, of external reality don't actually match the details of that reality.

- We feel inside of our head. Our feelings, however passionate and righteous they may be, are not only inside our head, they are *triggered* inside our head. Whatever it is out there that we are so upset about, it did not, and it never could, trigger our feelings or set their intensity. This all happens inside our head.

- The world we live in is inside of our heads. Certainly, as physical beings, our bodies live in physical reality, but our idea, our understanding, of physical reality exists entirely inside of our head, and has no defined relation to what actually exists outside of us beyond what our reproducible tests prove is real.

Yes, the physical world really does exist outside of our head, but our understanding of it exists nowhere but inside our head. But, this won't stop you from trying to tell me the truth of how the world *really* is, or how people *really* are, even though a little humility is surely in order.

Yes, we need decisiveness in order to make decisions and to take timely actions, but while in the consideration phase — where we spend most of our time — surely it is not asking too much to expect you to be able to acknowledge that almost all of your ideas about reality are untested notions whose only justification is that you are comfortable with them and they link you to your friends and colleagues.

LAW 3: Cognition is evaluation based

Cognition is evaluation-based, not knowledge-based. Aided by the purblind defect, we have this inherent assumption and expectation that our mind exists to gather knowledge and to understand whatever it surveys. By now I hope that you have some appreciation of how ridiculous this assumption is. How could that ever be reconciled with evolution and mortality? The thought that we spend everyday perfecting our knowledge of reality because that is what the mind is built for, what it does, is just too silly to imagine. The ability to know the inner truth of external things does not even enter into the discussion of abilities that can be transmitted genetically.

We are mortal beings who are built to use movement to enhance our survival chances, so we naturally evaluate everything in terms of our own needs and vulnerabilities. We are not built to learn, or to care, about what things are in their own right. As mobile creatures, we survive to the extent that we are good at assessing what things mean to us, how they impact our interests. Being able to perceive the needs and ambitions of a random animal crossing our path has nothing to do with it.

L0 and L1 are not anachronistic, as many of our moral guides have argued in the past, and even today. The answer to our problems is *not* to eschew self-interest for the sake of peace with others. The lower level intellects contribute fully and effectively to the sum of the functionality that comes together to make our mind what it is, and what it should be. Trying to turn these lower mental levels off would neither work nor improve our behavior or morality. On the contrary, it would cause our evaluation-based cognitive systems to fail. Only by learning how L0 and L1 work, what their roles are, what their strengths and limitations are, can we even begin to understand how our mind, as a whole, works.

LAW 4: Evaluation is at least tripolar

In the UCM, the tripolarity of evaluation is modeled in the evacule, but there is nothing prohibiting a model from adding additional dimensions to evaluation if it proves to be viable and productive. The reason evaluation cannot have less than 3 dimensions is because no combination of the anti-self and pro-self dimensions alone can adequately model alienation and boredom, objectively observed attributes of cognitive response. In order for the model to be viable, it must have a third dimension to represent the non-self attribute.

LAW 5: Perception is reductive

You might think that perception exists to `perceive`, but not only is this not true, it doesn't even make any sense.

Think about it, you have a sensory organ, the eye, that receives waveforms from the environment, so ask yourself, what happens to those waveforms? Are they all stored, as is, like a video recording? Is the storage space for these waveforms infinite? Since they are being stored in our head, the answer is obviously no, not everything we see can be recorded in high resolution and stored in our head. But we already knew this, because we now know that the basis of cognition is evaluation, not knowledge, and this tells us all we need to know: the function of the perceptual system in animals is not to record reality, but to reduce the most important elements in perceptions of reality down to terms that can be evaluated.

The goal of perception is not to *see* so much as it is to *focus*, to ignore the unimportant in order to fix on the important. Our peripheral vision, for example, cannot see color, but is very good at sensing motion, the greatest source of threat. Perception is reductive because perception only exists to feed evaluations of attributes into the overall evaluation process that combines and simplifies those evaluations down into the format required for the mind to calculate the approach/retreat/ignore command sent to the body.

Perception reduces boundless sensory input down into

impressions of attributes that might have significance for us. It is an illusion created by both the purblind defect and the misplaced position of our conscious mind in our mental structure that makes us think that we have the equipment to perceive reality as it is. We are mortal beings who cannot survive a break of more than a few seconds in our consumption of the necessaries of life. This means that our senses have to interpret experience into survival relevant terms in real time so that we can use movement to assure our survival. There is no time to get distracted by irrelevant details. The fact that distraction is a major cause of fatal accidents only proves this to be so.

The function of perception is to reduce the endless detail in the things out there down into a form that we can evaluate according to our mortality interests. Perception discards data that doesn't correspond to attributes we consider significant.

Even though our human brain evidently does have some capacity to store unexamined images that we can access and review later, this underused ability does not seem to factor heavily into the survival equation, and seems to be more of an accident of mutation that might be more useful in the future, after more new abilities are grouped with it, than it is right now.

LAW 6: Error exceeds content

It shouldn't be difficult to understand that the limited volume of our skull places a constraint on how much data can be stored, but when you add in the fact that the data is retained to support evaluation rather than knowledge, you can easily see that data storage is necessarily a parsimonious process. Add in the fact that every detail of every object and event we commit to memory has to be individually stored and recalled, and you can see that the effort and the space needed to store data about something is at least proportional to the amount stored.

If we flip to the other side and look at the number of details and measurements that could be taken for any object by including all available scales and perspectives from the macro to the subatomic levels, we can see that there is an unbounded amount of information that could be stored for anything. But, we never collect, let alone store, all of that information, and in general, only retain as much data as we need for our purposes.

This means that, in all cases, the difference between our idea of a thing, and the amount of data that could be gotten from the thing, i.e., the error between idea and thing, is always greater than the amount of data we have in any idea.

Objecting that these details don't matter is not a persuasive argument. On the contrary, it makes the point: you know only as much about a thing as you deem to be important for your needs and interests. It is precisely because organic cognition is evaluation-based, rather than knowledge-based, that the variance, the error, between idea and thing is always greater than the amount of data in the idea.

If nothing else, what you should take away from this law is a reminder that presuming beyond your competence is unwise, so maybe we should humble up just a bit.

Chapter 4

Realities

Reality, at least physical reality, is just about as simple as you think it is. It's only academics who try to make it difficult. I mean, if you can touch it, it's real; if it can hurt you, it's real. There's not much to get confused by, but intellectuals manage to do just that because they don't know that we think inside of our heads. Being ignorant of this elementary, self-evident fact causes them to confuse their *idea* of a thing with the *thing* itself, and then, when they notice that different people have different ideas about the same thing, they draw the only wrong conclusion they possibly could: it's not the idea of the thing that's fuzzy and subjective, they conclude, it's the thing itself that is somehow subjective.

Idiots.

But, on the off chance that you find yourself in an argument with one of these flakes sometime in the future, I'm going to give you both the formal definition of reality, and the missing key model that is needed to understand reality without getting your ideas all knotted together. Once you wrap your head around these two things, you'll be able to help poor benighted intellectuals unconfuse themselves enough to where they will finally be able to tie their own shoes. Sometimes.

So, let's start with the formal definition of reality:

Reality: an isolated set of elements and the means
by which they interact.

The key word here is `isolated`: the elements in a reality can't be affected by anything outside of the reality; only forces within that reality can have an impact. By `impact`, we mean a measurable, predictable impact. Physical reality, for example, is made up of all the atomic components we know about, and the forces listed in the standard model (strong force, weak force, etc.). Scientists have realized that the standard model is missing some elements and forces because their calculated predictions don't match their observations. But, this just means that there is more to learn, more stuff to add to the definition of physical reality, so it doesn't affect this discussion in the least.

From a practical point of view, physical reality is the set of all measurables: if it's in physical reality, it can be measured, and if it can be measured, it's in physical reality (roughly speaking). If it has mass or physical force, if you can touch it or measure it, either by hand or with an instrument, then it's real in physical reality.

It would be just that simple, and the discussion could end right here, if only it weren't for the missing key concept mentioned earlier. The first step we have to take to understand the missing key model is to think about the following sentence for a moment.

Ideas are an artifact of evaluation.

This means that, while organic entities live in physical reality, *ideas only exist in the mind of organic entities that can evaluate perceptions.* Furthermore, ideas can only achieve full meaning in the context of their mortality perspective, since value and context only exist as evaluations in our mind. In other words, **ideas don't exist in physical reality**, they only exist in mental reality, and they only manifest in physical reality when the idea is transformed into a physical action, and then its the action that happens/exists in physical reality, not the idea.

Is it a surprise that ideas don't exist in physical reality?

I don't think so, even though you may never have taken the time to ponder it before now. After all, what do a rock and the idea of a rock have in common? In a word, nothing. A rock is made of matter, an idea is an abstraction whose meaning depends on language.

So, this means that ideas exist in a language-based reality (ideas are expressed in language) that supports communication-based social groups (we learn language from a group). While the ideas do exist inside our head, we learn the language that forms and expresses them from communication with our community.

The implication of this is that words, ideas, and social relations exist in a **different** reality than animals, rocks, and wind do. This other reality is called `semantic reality`, because it's the reality of meaning, not of things. The elements in this reality include both the social (but not physical) side of us that interacts with others, and the messages that we pass back and forth to create and sustain social, work, and institutional associations. This is where groups, language, customs, and cultures exist.

Our physical bodies exist in physical reality, but not our thoughts, they exist in a separate reality[1] because there is no event in physical reality that can cause a partic-

---

[1] See *Ultrareasoning* for a detailed explanation of cognitive space, $\mathbb{CS}, \xi$, and the formal definition of $\mathbb{SR}$.

ular event, e_i, to happen in semantic reality. Not everyone responds to a clap of thunder in the same way, and not all people in a vicinity will even hear it.

Where physical reality is the set of all measurables, semantic reality is the set of all relationship forces that govern grouping in a species of cognitive entities. Where physical reality can be measured, semantic reality can be observed and simulated when it is quantitatively modeled.

Reality can kill you, but it can't make you say *pickle*. Enemies can torture you into saying it (sometimes, not all the time, it depends on the victim), but they can't do this without the *intention* of doing it, and while actions do happen in physical reality, intentions only exist in semantic reality. Like any other idea, intention cannot be formed in physical reality, it can only reference physical reality through an idea formed in a mind. The mind is an emergent property of brain function, it arises from the interaction of mental functions, not directly from brain structure itself, so it is not a component of the brain itself. Ideas can only exist in the mind where they are produced.

Is it odd to say that semantic reality, the reality of intangible ideas, feelings, and relations, is an actual reality on par with physical reality? First of all, once you understand the definition of reality, then it is clear that semantic reality is a separate reality. End of discussion. But, more importantly, how does the word/idea of a rock fit into the same reality as a physical rock? Real rocks are made up of minerals, which are made up molecules, which are made up of atoms, which interact with each other and physical reality through physical forces. How does an idea, which exists only in the mind, and can only be communicated in words and images created by social interactions, and has no atoms, be in the same reality as a stone rock? Ideas are not made of the same stuff that things in physical reality are. Yes, the memory of the idea is imprinted on a physical structure, but the meaning of the idea only exists in a reality of meaning created by communication between individuals and groups.

Try thinking about this for a few minutes, and you should find that a lot of confusion about what reality is will start to melt away. Physical things exist in physical reality; idea, meaning, and relationship things exist in semantic reality. Physical reality can kill the brain from which the mind arises, but it cannot force a meaning or comprehension event to occur in a mind, because these things do not exist in physical reality, there is no counterpart in physical reality for value, meaning, self, or intention.

One of the great insights that the postmodernists infesting universities proclaim, is that "reality has no meaning!" The proper response to this is, "Watermelon has no broccoli. What's your point?" Of course, meaning does not exist in physical reality, because it only exists in semantic reality. Just as you shouldn't look for physical stones in the world of ideas and meaning, so you shouldn't look for meaning in the world of physical stones.

However, while the concept of reality is as simple as you expect, once you accept that there is more than one reality,[2] there's a little hitch that makes *talking* about it both difficult and confusing. When we refer to reality, we almost cannot help but think that we are referring to the real world out there, when, of course, what we are really talking about is the model we have of it inside our mind since `we think inside of our head`. It's sometimes very hard to keep the idea of reference vs. referent straight, particularly when we only really care about the latter.

There are two major problems that make these conversations confusing: 1) the indirection problem, and 2) the verification problem.

------

[2]More than two, actually, but that's a story for another day.

address	value	name	expression	explanation
3795480305	10	n	int n = 10	create integer variable n, set value to 10, operating system finds a place for it in memory at position 3795480305
	3795480305	ptr	int *ptr = &n	create an int type pointer, give it the address of n (&n)
			n == 10	n equals 10 as intended
			&n == 3795480305	the memory address of n is 3795480305
			ptr == 3795480305	the value in the pointer variable ptr is 3795480305, same as the address of n
			*ptr == 10	the value referenced by the pointer ptr is 10

Figure 4.1: Indirection

The indirection problem is caused by the fact that, no matter what we intend, we are always talking about a reference to the thing, instead of about the thing itself, even when we don't realize it. The best way that I can think of explaining why this is so confusing is to use an example from C programming. This example is as simple and straightforward as I can make it, yet I know that it will seem unnecessarily confusing to the non-programmers in the room, but that's the point. The takeaway you should get from the example below is a little dizziness from the confusion, not clarity. And please, do not struggle to clear that up, because it's the confusion, not clarity, that we're trying to illustrate.

In figure 4.1, we declare a variable named **n**, and assign it a value of 10. The operating system manages memory, and it puts **n** in some memory location that we are showing as 3795480305. So, the value of **n**, 10, is stored in location 3795480305. So far, so good.

Next, we create a pointer to an integer value, `ptr`, and assign it the value of the address of **n**, **&n**. So, the value of `ptr` is 3795480305. **n** still equals 10, and its address is still 3795480305. So, the value of `ptr` is 3795480305, but the value referenced by `ptr` (*ptr) is 10. Clear? Probably not.

See, it's easy to understand that **n** has the value of 10, and we don't care what its address is, so when we talk about it, we know that **n** = 10, and that's all that counts. But when we talk about `ptr`, its value is the address we don't care about, because what we care about is not `ptr`, but what `ptr` is referencing, which is 10. It's not that this is difficult to understand, it's just that the extra step between `ptr` and 10 can seem, and sometimes be, confusing, even to programmers.

It's roughly the same issue when we are talking about either of the two realities, physical or semantic, because what we're almost always interested in is what our models refer to, the world outside of us, not the internal model itself. So, when we talk about reality, we are referring to what's outside of us, but the only thing we can ever talk about is just the model inside of our head. Obviously, we care about the world out there, and the model in here is just a means to get to it, but we invariably lose sight of the distinction between the idea and the thing once we get deep into reasoning about it.

This brings us to the second issue, the verification problem. This really makes rigorous conversation difficult. To explain this, let's first imagine that there is a thing in external reality, and for argument's sake, let's imagine it's a really simple object like a square something, but all we care about is the shape. So, you form an idea of that square in your mind, and the question becomes: does that square you are thinking about exist in external reality? I mean, you supposedly got the idea *from* reality, so the idea should resemble the reality, wouldn't you think?

The first step in figuring out whether our internal idea actually maps to an external object is to convert our idea to a model by making it quantifiable and impersonal. Then, we pick a point on the square to test against reality. Leveraging our experience with jigsaw puzzles, we start with a corner point and test to see if we can measure the location of that corner in external reality. After we succeed in doing that, then if possible, we get an independent observer to repeat the test to verify our findings.

If the existence of that point is verified, then we might

repeat the process to get the other three corner points verified. Then, we have to ask ourselves, is this good enough to prove the square exists? From a practical or geometric point of view, it might be, but from a rigorous point of view, we would need much more than that. We would have to call out and verify many more points to ensure that it's not some other kind of regular polygon. At some point, we might decide that we are satisfied with our answer. Does this prove that our idea of a square perfectly represents the physical object? No, not really, because we haven't excluded the possibility that we are in an irregular problem space where the shape could be irregular and highly complex instead of a simple polygon. In other words, we saw a square, but on closer, or microscopic, inspection, maybe it's really a four sided squiggly.

So, can we finally know whether or not our internal ideas represent a true picture of the external thing? Still not really, because we haven't specified the acceptable margin of error we can allow between idea and thing, nor of the scale at which we will judge that tolerance. There's a big difference between "good enough for government work" and "good enough for space flight".

We're not playing games here; when we get all agitated and scream that our idea of reality is better than someone else's, what we're really doing is asserting that our way of seeing the world, which means our way of being, is the right way. If we were actually talking about measurable correlation between model and referent, then we would have a list with data points, a margin of error, and a scale that we could swap with each other so that we could verify each other's claim. But there's no emotion in measurement, and where's the fun, the excitement, and the screaming, in that?

Summary

Is reality subjective? No, certainly not. However, our internal *understanding* of everything, including realities, is subjective. The whole reason the scientific method had to be invented was to give us a robust, repeatable way to verify which of our ideas accurately describe something in physical reality, and which ones are just internal ideas. The fact that ideas in our head are subjective is hardly shocking.

Physical reality is simple, once you separate semantic reality from it. And, even though semantic reality is actually more complex than physical reality, it, too, is easier to understand once you separate the realities.

To answer our topic question, yes, reality does objectively exist, or more properly, realities do exist. But, as with any idea, `error exceeds content`, so the difference between our idea of reality and the external reality itself far exceeds what little we think we know about it.

Here's one thing you can take away from this chapter: ideas are not rocks, even when they are very hard, and well formed.

Chapter 5

Truth

Truth is a compass. We can use it to stay on course with a plan — be it a moral, economic, or lifestyle one — or to stay on task. We clearly stand a better chance of achieving our goals when our decisions are aligned with our plan.

Of course, we can decide that truth is nothing more than the scent of the next pleasure, the next big opportunity, or the next escape from responsibility. It's up to us.

In either case, truth is a compass that we use to find our way, however well- or ill-considered it may be. But, truth is not static. Even when sailing east and west across the oceans, compasses traditionally had to be periodically adjusted to keep giving correct readings, since magnetic north and true north are not the same thing.

The same principle holds true with whatever ideas or goals we use to guide our journey. Since we sometimes have to tack, to turn away from our course, in order to stay on it, we need a reliable guide of some kind to find our way back to it.

In a universe in which life and cognition evolves, why do we suppose that our inborn notion of a simple right/ wrong truth test works equally well for all intellects and all realities? Wouldn't it make more sense if each reality had its own truth test? In fact, how could tangible, physical reality have the same truth test as semantic reality, the reality of the intangible?

Now that we know about multiple realities and multiple intellect levels, our understanding of truth has to evolve, at least a little. Each reality has to have its own truth test simply because the things and relations that exist in one reality don't exist in the other, so no test for truth could be valid in both. This goes for intellect levels also. Since each level of the intellect has a different data structure, surely it's obvious that there has to a different truth test for each one.

The common admonition that "not everything is black and white" comes from us all realizing that life is sometimes too complicated to fit neatly into a simple right or wrong bucket. But, if everything isn't as simple as right or wrong, then what is it?

Truth *is* real, and not everything is relative, but what happens if the true/false dichotomy, which we rely on to know the difference between right and wrong, isn't universal, but is just a special case in the larger scheme of things? Now that we know about the various realities and levels of intellect, mightn't we suspect that the true/false solution is only one of several kinds of truth that apply in different situations?

It wouldn't be the first time we found out that something we thought was true everywhere, was really only true in one type of situation. Relativity showed us that `time` itself is not constant, but varies with velocity. This affects us everyday, since our GPS systems wouldn't work if we didn't know that time moves a little slower at our satellites than it does for us on earth. For another example, we all know that parallel lines don't cross, but they can in non-Euclidean geometry. We found out that this wasn't just an exercise in abstraction once general relativity showed us that space-time is distorted by matter.

If you're doing the math on how many different truth functions we need for 4 levels of intellect and 2 realities, it is $4 * 2 = 8$ potentially different truth tests.[1] Worriest thou not, though, for you will see that when we take them on one at a time, they all turn out to be pretty simple and obvious, and they don't invalidate our fundamental notion of true and false and right and wrong. And, there's no quiz at the end, so you can relax.

Think back to the definition of a reality: an isolated set of elements and the means by which they interact. By definition, there simply has to be different truths for different realities. A serious test of truth is demonstrated in physical reality by death and natural selection, and the scientific method gives us another test that proves whether or not our ideas about physical reality are correct. On the other hand, in semantic reality, truth is demonstrated by the capacity of a message to change a group's power, and consequently, its ability to access resources.

Truth In Physical Reality

Because we think inside of our head, and cannot know the world directly, our *experience* of physical reality is subjective, but this does not even begin to suggest to the intelligent mind that *reality*, itself, is subjective. There is

---

[1]See *Super Stupid* for an extended discussion on this that covers 12 different truth functions.

nothing subjective about the scientific method's ability to test truth in physical reality. The discipline of the method enables us to verify, within a margin of error, that a particular phenomenon referenced by an idea actually exists in the reality outside of our mind. It does this by having multiple observers independently measure the same phenomenon with the same method. The prediction that x behaves in such-and-such a way, within a margin of error, is validated when the experiment is run a sufficient number of times by independent observers, because it proves that they are all observing the same thing in the common reality outside of their head.

Why do we need the scientific method? Since `we think inside of our head`, we need the discipline of the scientific method to be able to differentiate between ideas that exist only internally in our brain, and those that accurately refer to something that actually exists outside of us.

However, because `error exceeds content`, the objectivity of reality doesn't guarantee that, even with the scientific method on our side, all of our ideas about reality are absolutely right to any significant extent. A reproducible test may verify a dozen points in our model, but that does not in any way imply that the unmeasured points in reality match the other ideas in our head, or even that our ideas include any of the most important facets of the real object.

So, while the scientific method does give us the ability to verify that a limited number of the data points in our internal model do, in fact, exist in external reality, it does not, in any way, make us experts on reality, or give us the ability to know anything beyond our few rigorously proven facts.

Truth In Semantic Reality

Gravity can disappoint us when the ice cream scoop falls off of our cone onto the ground; it can hurt, or even kill us when we fall off a mountain, or even a ladder. Does our recognition of the law of gravity mean that we *want* gravity to be what it is, or that we *support* it being that way? Of course not, we are just observing and understanding what has been, is, and will be, in a particular reality that is entirely independent of us.

And so it is with truth in semantic reality. You might find the following explanation of truth to be morally objectionable, but if you honestly search history and your own personal experience, you will eventually have to reluctantly agree that what I am going to describe is exactly what you have observed. This doesn't mean that I am recommending it, or that I approve of it, just that I am trying to rigorously describe how semantic reality actually works.

The formula for truth in semantic reality is discussed elsewhere,[2] but here's how it works in simple terms: groups are made up of the social part of people, the messages they share, and the consequences of resulting actions. The truth of a message is measured by how much it strengthens or weakens the social bonds in the group, or how much it affects resource distribution. That's it.

What this definition of truth in semantic reality means, is that what a message in semantic reality claims about physical reality has *absolutely nothing to do* with its truth value in semantic reality. A lie about physical reality can be, and often is, completely true in semantic reality. Whether the lie about physical reality ever comes back to bite the liar or his listeners is completely immaterial. Think about it. Physical reality and semantic reality are two different realities, that means that what happens in one cannot directly cause a specific result in the other.

We have all been lied to by salespeople determined to sell us whatever they have, instead of what we need. We have all seen politicians on all sides tell us that their poli-

---

[2]$t \propto \frac{|G'+m|}{|G'|}$, see *Ultrareasoning*.

cies will improve life for everybody, and society in general, when we know that to be impossible. Yet, the lie works well enough to swell the ranks of their party sufficiently to win them the election. Reprehensible, you say? Maybe, but truth in semantic reality is proportional to the ability of the group to distort the resource landscape in a way that causes additional resources to be drawn into the group's ambit.

Still don't like it? This is wrong, you say? Resources should be distributed according to need or merit? The weakest and least powerful should get first portions? Fine, but only groups can attempt to create that reality, and the power of the group distorts the geometry of the space in semantic reality in such a way that resources flow down hill towards the functionaries at the center of the group. Thus, the spoils will go to the benefit of the controlling party, not to the deserving poor, or any other outsiders, who will remain, or become, poor. Whether the party deigns to redistribute some of its newly acquired wealth outside of the party apparatus is a completely separate question.

But, you claim, it would be different if you were in charge. To make that true, you would first have to deal with the fact that, just as gravity is the force responsible for the larger structures in physical reality, group power is the force responsible for the larger structures, such as societies and civilizations, in semantic reality. So, this means that the first thing you would have to do to establish your utopia is to change the laws of nature, and, as long as we are going to revoke the laws of semantic reality, why not revoke those of physical reality at the same time, and get rid of gravity?

Revoking the laws of reality is a losing proposition, but since our knowledge of such laws is subjective, it is true that not every so-called law is necessarily a real law. However, discriminating between the two would require a rigorous journey of exploration and discovery, and that requires L3 level query skills that are well beyond the meager limits of a university education. So, that's not gonna be happening in our lifetime.

Eight or Nine Different Kinds of Truth

Nine different kinds of truth are listed below, instead of the promised eight, because one of the eight has been split into two to make it easier to understand. The goal of this discussion is not to move you off of absolute truth into the land of relative values, but simply to explain the different ways that the mind calculates truth on its different levels in the different realities, regardless of whether you like it or not, or even acknowledge it. Ask yourself, which would you prefer: to be impotently befuddled and frustrated every time you see a group of people get bigger and stronger because their leader lies to them, or would you be better off if you saw it coming and understood the mechanism well enough to maybe do something about it?

We will start by examining the most abstract and least familiar truth, L3, in both physical reality and semantic reality, and then proceed down through the levels, finishing with absolute truth, the truth that many of us think is the only real one.

L3 Truth

Truth in level L3 is abstract and unknown to almost everyone. The reason it is so rare is that it is the truth of model building, not of an external or internal reality. The goal of model building is to craft a formal, executable model that can be tested against its target reality. This means that there are two levels of truth in model building: 1) the truth that guides the *assembly* of the model, and 2) the truth of *testing* the model.

The truth that governs the testing of the model is

that of the scientific method, so that doesn't require further explanation. The truth that governs the assembly and creation of the model has two parts: `viability` and `productivity`, and this merits some attention.

The `viable` facet of L3 truth is an informal test of the model against reality (either physical or semantic) to see whether reality obviously contradicts the idea. We can use an informal truth test at this point in model assembly because all we are doing is trying to connect ideas with other ideas to temporarily bridge a gap for just long enough to get to the other side to continue our trek to the next gap. Once the model is fully assembled we formally test it, so any undue liberties we take in the early steps will be caught then. The risk of wasting effort is more than recompensed by the possibility of finding hidden potential, which is pretty likely given that `error exceeds content`, so there is always hidden potential in our models.

The `productive` facet of L3 truth is also an informal test, it tests whether our ability to generate hypotheses increases or decreases when we connect a new idea to our model.

As explained in *General Problem Theory*, faceted model-oriented reasoning is a method that supports exploration of the unknown, so it is only to be expected that its principles should seem specialized and unusual, because they are. The thing to remember is that L3 truth is merely provisional, and the real test happens once the model is complete enough to be subjected to more conventional tests whose results are reproducible and durable.

L2 Truth

L2 truth is social truth, the truth that sustains the group, and which the group reinforces. You can think of it as the truth of spoken and written word ideas, of messages exchanged between people. Even though we spend most of our time thinking word thoughts silently inside our head, this is a social activity because we learned the words from our society, and we can only communicate our ideas in words to other people. A language known only to one person means exactly nothing until it is shared by others, and only after it becomes the medium of social interaction will it grow enough to be able to describe the complexities of life.

Three of the nine different forms of truth are included in L2 truth: **narrativized**, **consistency**, and **group** truths.

5. Narrativized

The **narrativized** truth function assigns an L0 truth value to a current or remembered event at the time it's inserted into an L2 narrative, i.e., the reality-based event is embedded in a meaningful narrative, greatly expanding its significance. The new truth value comes from the narrative and overwrites the original truth value. This means that the truth value we assign to real, experienced events merely by embedding them into an L2 idea framework disconnects them from their original reality basis, and redefines them to fit with our personal or group value system, regardless of how silly and unrealistic it may be.

We see the effect of this whenever a small action or event is suddenly invested with an outsized significance, because meaning is less in the observed action, than it is injected into it by the mechanism we use to infuse our life with significance, which is whatever personal, political, ideological, or religious narrative we choose to use.

The narrative is a story with a long arc that ties the events in our life together — whether they are actually related or not — into a theme that matches our self-concept and experience of life. Because L2 is built to interpret everything in terms of patterns, our mind prefers to interpret our life as part of a story, even if it's a tragic one, rather than to see it as a meaningless series of unrelated events.

Thus, narrativized truth can replace the truth previously assigned to an event during an actual experience in external reality, with an abstract, intellectual truth that is based on largely untested ideas, rather than experience. The results are sometimes strange and inexplicable to non-cult members.

If this sounds kind of murky and confusing, it's because it is: narrativized truth can be, and often is, objectively false, but to those inside the group, it remains stubbornly true for as long as their determination can sustain it.

6. Consistency, Logic, Grammar

The `consistency` truth function validates an idea or statement by checking it for consistency with some self-defined logic or grammar rules, or group norms. Consistency is the most intellectually respected form of truth, but it is nevertheless the weakest and least reliable test of truth. Consistency only checks against L2 language-based rules, instead of against either measurement or reality. The primary function of consistency truth is to maintain an equilibrium with an existing mindset, or group alliance structure, as opposed to verifying an idea against an external reality.

The convenient thing about consistency truth is that each person not only gets to define which rules are included in the check, but also whether or not the idea passes the tests. This standard for truth is so flexible that ideas can even be validated against undefined tests. You have to admit that's convenient.

7. Group

The **group** truth function applies known or anticipated group ideas or doctrines to determine the truth or falsity of an idea. Sometimes mistakes are made, but the intention is to assess the idea in the same way that the group's leaders would. The purpose of the group truth function is to maintain or strengthen one's current connections with the group.

Being able to correctly anticipate unarticulated group judgment on new situations often results in an improvement in one's position within the group. So, the motivation for following group truth is to maintain one's prerogatives in the group structure, while the reward for anticipating group truth can be an enhancement of one's power within the group.

L2 Truth Summary

L2 truth is the truth of the group, and of the set of small rules we acknowledge (such as informal logic, or even etiquette) that govern the validity of connecting ideas together into a whole that defines our worldview.

L2 evaluates messages by interpreting the linguistic meaning in them, and then evaluating the message down into the L0 truth structure, regardless of whether the message content is physics or gossip. The intensity of L2 truth is determined by the L0 truth that we assign to the idea, but the evaluation decision is often determined by how important it is for us to share this opinion with the concerned group, whether it be family, friends, colleagues, or fellow party members.

L1 Truth

L1 truth is the truth of experience, of authority. It is the voice that tells us to follow the decision already made, to reject exploration and experimentation in favor of sticking to known pathways. The truth of experience is based on a simple comparison of the situation before an action to the situation after it, to determine whether the action helped or hurt our interests.

Deference to authority is essentially the same thing as deference to experience, the only difference being that we are deferring to the experience of another, instead of to our own, a habit we can pick up from obeying our parents.

L1 is a relatively modest extension of L0 in that the major difference is the comparison used in evaluation operates on structures in memory instead of just perceptions. But, learning from experience is a huge advancement in cognitive ability and viability enhancement.

While learning from experience in physical reality is taken for granted, and can be observed in all creatures large and small, since L1 creatures can be social, it is not surprising that L1 also enables us to learn from social experiences (L1 in semantic reality). This is how young animals learn the social cues involved in hierarchy and cooperation. From a memory point of view, apart from being able to observe and understand messages sent by posture, gesture, and sound, there is not much difference between learning from experiences in physical and semantic realities. In both cases, the pre and post situations are compared to evaluate the lesson as positive or negative.

In both cases, the intensity of the truth learned from the lesson is related to our ability to sense, from action or behavior, the severity of the risk that ignoring the lesson might entail. Semantic reality transgressions are often punished in physical reality, but since not everyone learns the intended lesson, this is just another example of the separation of the realities.

L0 Truth

Absolute

Most folks think that absolute truth is the only real, legitimate truth. Absolute truth is all about two choices: right/wrong, good/evil, go/no-go, right/left. Absolute truth is the whole world reduced to two choices, right or wrong. Even when it's hard for us to figure out whether some particular action is right or wrong, we are usually pretty sure it is definitely one or the other.

Unless they actually make an effort to think about it, most people seem to assume that absolute truth is actually a permanent, built-in part of nature, and that some, or most, things in reality are inherently **good** or **bad**. The absolute nature of absolute truth actually comes from the fact that it represents our mortality interests, because if we die, the world ends for us, which, you must agree, is pretty absolute. It represents the truth of natural selection that forms our genetic blueprint, the truth of the harshness of physical reality, and of our ultimate vulnerability to even the smallest shock in the wrong circumstance.

Natural selection is the basis of L0 truth because organisms that cannot properly discriminate between threat and opportunity will soon fail to survive in numbers sufficient to propagate their species. The quintessential example of genetically transmitted absolute truth is that big, loud, carnivorous things running towards us are absolutely bad, just as fresh water and wholesome food are absolutely good. Over time, survivors are selected by their behavioral conformance to the brute realities of their environment, so their ideas of good and bad naturally conform to their local reality, too.

Thus, L0 truth is an external standard that is imposed on a species by natural selection, and it equates to a calculation of the likelihood that a species will survive in a particular type of environment. It's safe to say that there is not a lot of philosophy in L0 truth in physical reality. On the contrary, L0 truth is better and higher than that, since it's entirely grounded in reality.

The key attribute in L0 absolute truth is that it is directly *actionable*: L0 truth can always be used to make a decision, and can always be acted on. Absolute truth provides the emotional certainty, the conviction, that enables you go forth and confront the risks and terrors of life, because it has the same form as the decision structure. L0 truth is absolute in the sense that it just is, it is not arrived at by debate, it is the source of truth. Even degrees of absolute truth are above argument, because, in defining ultimate right and wrong, ideas with the characteristic of the absolute are the standard by which everything else is judged.

Truth is determined by the L0 intellect in the context of physical reality — the only reality it knows — by taking what our sensory organs tell us and comparing that to the archetypal patterns of all-good to all-bad (and every combination in between) inherited in our genotype, to produce an evaluation that maps directly to an action command.

The tripolar evaluation of good/bad/indifferent is the basis of our emotions of love, hate, and alienation or indifference, and of all of our critical reasoning, morality, and judgment. While this fundamental level of truth is important and indispensable — it is the junction we have to go through in order to *act* — it is not the only truth.

Assigned Absolute

This is the big, hairy truth that governs most of our life, even though you've never heard of it. Assigned absolute truth is the mechanism that enables us to hook up different levels of emotional power to any idea we want to push. While an argument can be made for the importance and validity of absolute truth, since it is the voice of natural selection, **assigned absolute truth** is a whole other beast.

Assigned absolute truth comes into play when we evaluate things people say or do to us, things that happen to us, things that we read, see, or hear. We correlate the idea or message with other things we know and feel, and decide that, for example, it was an insult, and then we let it fester for a while and finally decide it was the worst insult ever. This is how an innocent remark can sometimes set off a conflagration of recriminations that can destroy relationships, families, and communities.

Assigned absolute truth has the power of absolute truth, with none of pedigree of actual experience. Our higher intellect, L2, *chooses* to assign absolute truth to something for whatever reason it wants. Whether we decide to assign it, or whether it is triggered automatically, as sometimes can happen, the decision to accept it is entirely within our conscious control.

L2 has access to the lower level circuits of the mind, plus it has the adolescent arrogance to use the power of

L0 truth on a whim. This is why we can react to a verbal slight the same way we react to a physical attack. The key difference between assigned and absolute truth is that we get to do the assignment ourselves, instead of relying on eons of natural selection to do it. To make it worse, there is no elder with the wisdom of experience to look over our shoulder and check our work, or to rein us in. We're free to label anything as maximum evil, for whatever reason, or for no reason at all.

Assigned absolute truth is a borrowed truth, assigned to abstract ideas and feelings by our choice. We decide what is unforgivable, what is just a slight, and what can be ignored altogether.

This does not mean that our assignments are always wrong or inappropriate, but you can be certain that they often are, and are sometimes utterly inexcusable.

Understand, we cannot live without assigned absolute truth, it is how we make ideas actionable, and there is no substitute for it, since impotently sitting on the sidelines refusing to make a decision is not a valid choice. The point in calling assigned absolute truth out is to draw attention to the fact that it is a different kind of truth than absolute truth is because we own it, we control the judgments that decide what is good and bad, as well as the judgment of just how good or bad something is.

Because we have no clue about any of this stuff, when we do assign an intense absolute truth to something, we mistakenly think that this is what the thing actually is, not just an evaluation we are putting on it. Both absolute and assigned absolute truth feel the same, since the L0 archetypal truth is the power behind both. However, with an intellectual understanding of the difference, we can have new options on assigning, recognizing, and responding to assigned absolute truth that we didn't have before.

Assigned absolute truth is the evaluation we add to higher level thought — or to which we reduce higher level thought — in order to be able to react decisively to events. We often feel like we don't fully understand higher level ideas until we can conclusively decide whether they are absolutely right or wrong or unimportant. This assignment of life and death truth to intangible feelings, words, actions, and intentions, is the critical link that connects abstract ideas and feelings to the perception-action process.

The curious thing about attaching assigned absolute truth to higher level thought is that it is both optional *and* necessary. It is optional because we have the option to defer the assignment of a visceral truth value, and to just accept, for the time being, that an idea is simply as true as the evidence supporting it indicates. But it's necessary that we ultimately assign a truth to an idea in order to be able to act decisively on it.

As long as an idea is held in an L2 'logical' evaluation state, we can have minimal emotional attachment or commitment to it. This is why eggheads and clerics have traditionally had the reputation of being feckless ivory tower intellectuals, because they wouldn't commit to practical ideas, preferring, instead, to remain aloof from the fray, as though their status put them above the messy, rough and tumble struggles of daily life. This has led men of action to often dismiss the concerns of ethicists as impractical, since the academic elite were artificially insulated from the pressures of competitive struggles, and hence insensitive to, or ignorant of, them.

Summary

The vast majority of our experience with truth is through assigned absolute truth that we control, but this is not what we feel. It usually seems that truth is beyond our control, that it is just what is, as decided by human, natural, or supernatural authority. We are often tyrannized by group truth when we know that we could be ostracized, or worse, from our work or social groups, if we were to express the wrong opinion.

But, nothing changes the fact that most of the ideas that frame our life are like fences we put up around a pasture when we assign absolute truth to an idea. They constrain us from exploring, rather than connect us to, possibilities.

No, we do not get to define truth in whatever way we want because external truths are measurable, and no, not all truth is relative, but truth is defined differently in different realities on different data structures. Physical reality is as real as life and death, and even semantic reality is real and its truth is real enough to have the power to predictably cause the death of millions in every generation.

What you should do with this information is up to you, but surely, by now you can see how silly it is to think that everything reduces to the simple true/false binary. Evolved life is more complicated than that.

Below is a little table that summarizes the major points of this chapter on truth. Do with it what you will.

Level/Reality	Truth Function
L0/$\mathbb{R}$	comparison to inherited archetypes
L0/$\mathbb{SR}$	evaluate intangibles as tangibles
L1/$\mathbb{R}$	personal evaluation of experience in $\mathbb{R}$
L1/$\mathbb{SR}$	personal evaluation of experience in $\mathbb{SR}$
L2/$\mathbb{R}$	evaluate $\mathbb{R}$ events as $\mathbb{SR}$ events
L2/$\mathbb{SR}_1$	logic and grammatical correctness
L2/$\mathbb{SR}_2$	message effect on group bond strength
L3/$\mathbb{R}$	robustness of idea to contradiction in $\mathbb{R}$
L3/$\mathbb{SR}$	query productivity of an idea

Table 5.1: Truth by Intellect Level and Reality

Part II

The Inner Workings

Chapter 6

Chaos and Loopbacks

A loopback is a saying, belief, or idea that's always true in any circumstance. Some are so true that they can trump all other ideas, experiences, hopes, and fears about the future. The term 'loopback' comes from electronic circuits that return unprocessed signals back to their source. In the mind, the loopback moves us away from obsessing about a hot possibility by calming and reassuring us with a little bit of wisdom or faith that, from a physical perspective, actually helps to drain excess charge off of an over-excited idea circuit.

Loopbacks can be based on serious theological or philosophical beliefs ("How unfathomable are his decisions and unexplainable are his ways!"), or they can spontaneously arise from the current jargon of the day ("Chill, dude!").

Some loopbacks can act as a doorway back into serious thought, while others just act like a blanket that smothers disquieting flames.

Loopbacks can seem like philosophy or theology on the cheap, sort of like fortune cookie wisdom that sounds incredibly simplistic and useless. Funny thing, though, is that loopbacks work — however silly they may sound — and the right one will immediately start to calm down your nervous thoughts. Not every loopback works for every person, of course, because they only work if you believe them on some level. Some have a lasting effect, while others have to be repeated like a mantra to be effective.

An even funnier thing about loopbacks is that there actually is a mathematical basis for them that not only explains why they work, but also why they are important and universal.

The L2 level of our mind endlessly processes both old and new patterns, almost regardless of what is going on around us at the time. Even when we are engaged in something as serious as driving, L2 will often be off in la-la land, entertaining itself by spinning out memories, stories, and scenarios for our private amusement. To be sure, when we suddenly find ourselves in a pinch, L2 will usually immediately stop daydreaming to engage with the problem at hand, perhaps by searching for any kind of pattern that might help us out of the immediate trouble.

Whenever we are confronted with anything of interest, be it a problem or an opportunity, our L2 rational mind will automatically search its memory for *any* patterns that sort of match the problem in question. We all experience this automatic search everyday in social and work settings. It shows up in phrases we hear and say: "that reminds me...", "that made me think of something...", "you know what might work...", and so on. Often, these remarks are followed by, "Uh, no, never mind, that wouldn't work", or "On second thought...", and the like, where, after a moment of reflection, we discard the low quality ideas that popped into our head.

However, when the ideas that pop into our head strike a chord of hope or dread deep in our soul, the L2 mind will start to run with those ideas, following them across their links to other ideas that link to still more ideas to see what kind of future can be anticipated. This generally fails to reach a satisfying conclusion, and the more emotionally triggering the idea is, the more our mood is altered by the worrying or tantalizing what-if exercise. Absent an interruption, our mind will often then go back to the beginning to run the whole exercise again, but with the significant difference that our emotional state has been altered by the previous journey into the realm of hope or fear.

It's important to understand that the data from our internal senses includes our emotional state, and this plays a critical role in the calculation of how to turn evaluation into action. The problem this causes is that now, when we rerun the anticipation function, we are using the output from the last run — our changed emotional state — as input to the next run. This is alarming, because it means that we have accidentally transformed our reasoning process into a feedback circuit.

The problem with feedback circuits is that they produce output that is inherently chaotic, and this holds true even in the circuits in our brain that produce thought. This chaos manifests as extreme emotional swings and unstable ideation that doesn't converge on clarity. People gripped by chaotic thinking for extended periods tend to become highly emotional, displaying such symptoms as anxiety, obsession, depression, or even restrained hysteria.

This is not just a problem, it's a huge problem that transcends our psychological, political, religious, philosophical, and social perspectives, because it originates below the level of our thoughts in the underlying organic/ structural layer, where only mathematical and mechanical analysis penetrates, and none of our higher level concepts apply.

The problem is that all functions that eat their own output generate chaos, and it makes no difference whether the function is mathematical, executable code, or cognitive. You may find it hard to believe that our thought process works the same way that electronic circuits do, but of course they do. To make it a little easier to see how this can lead to trouble, let's look at an example of what happens when a very simple function consumes its own output, and see how that applies to how our mind works.

Our example is a simple parabolic function of the type that you should recognize from school:

$$y = x^2 + x + 4$$

When we feed 101 integers ranging from -50 to 50 into the equation, one at a time, we get a list of values for y that are shown in figure 6.1, a nice parabola. Now, if we randomly sort these integers, we get a graph of the input to the function that will look something like figure 6.2, and a graph of the output of the function that will look like figure 6.3. These last two graphs look messy, but they just show randomness, not chaos. Notice that the scale on the

Chaos and Loopbacks

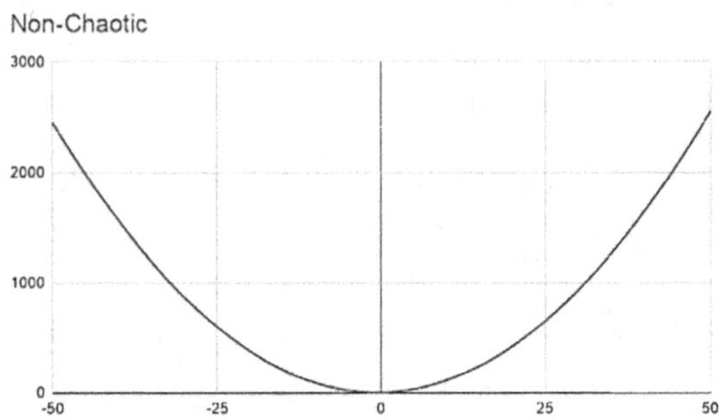

Figure 6.1: Normal, non-chaotic parabola

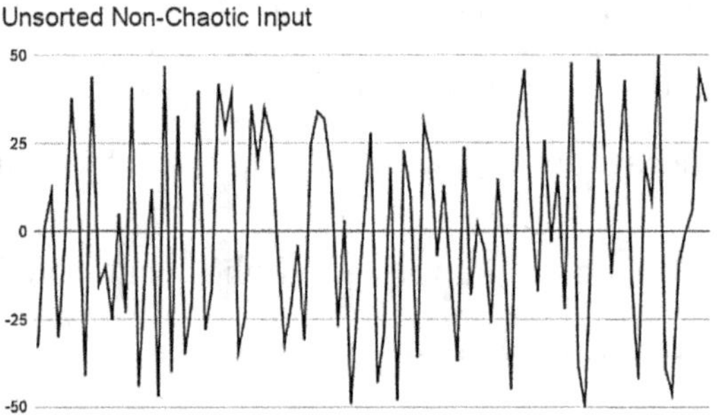

Figure 6.2: Graph of unsorted input

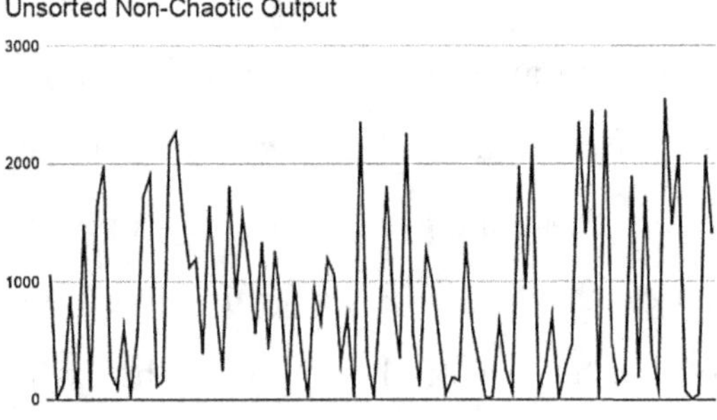

Figure 6.3: Graph of unsorted output

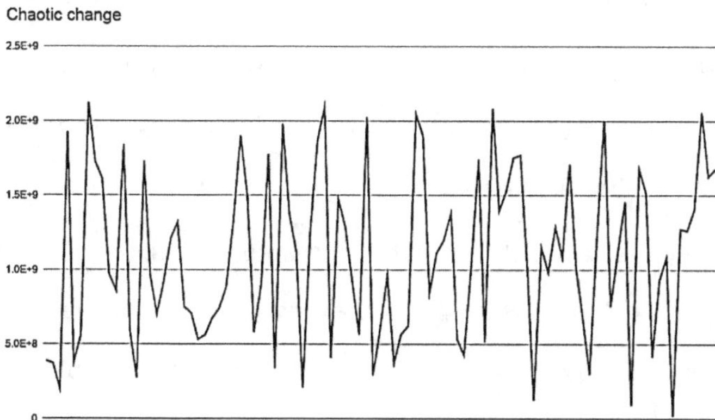

Figure 6.4: Feedback chaos

x and y axes in figure in figure 6.3 hasn't changed, and nothing has gotten weird or out of hand, just switched around. Figure 6.3 is a disordered graph, but it is not chaotic because it can be easily transformed back into the original shape with some simple sorting.

Figure 6.4, on the other hand, shows what happens when we feed the output from one step of the function back into it as input to the next step. Notice the scale on the y axis: instead of ranging from 0 to 3,000, the values in this chaotic graph range from 0 to 2,500,000,000. The swings in the graph are a million times greater than in the non-chaotic graph, and this was just caused by using the output from the previous cycle as the input for the next. It is worth noting that the swings are limited only by the integer size used in the calculations, and that using a larger size numerical data type would result in much larger values (up to 8,955,207,510,679,229,124 when long is used instead of integer).

Because the L2 pattern processing engine does nothing but process patterns all day, every day — both new and old ones — it is inherently subject to chaotic disturbances whenever it begins to continuously process its own output since that throws it into an uncontrolled feedback loop.

Feedback loops can be disrupted by loopbacks, because **loopbacks substitute their bromides in place of the previous output as input to the next cycle, thus breaking the feedback cycle that creates chaos.**

The way this works is that chaotic thought ensues when a chain of reasoning upsets us emotionally, **and** fails to reach a solution. This triggers the vicious cycle in which we fixate on searching for a solution while getting more and more anxious and desperate (or manic) each time through the process. A loopback contains some version of the *calm down* message that gets sent through the thought circuits instead of continuing to ramp up the anxiety provoked by the dread of a damnable outcome. The longer we can disrupt the original feedback cycle, the more the excited charge in it can drain off, and the quicker we can return to normal.

This chaos manifests as alienation, powerlessness, anxiety, depression, and fear. This is inherent in the design of L2. This is why we are taught to listen more to our betters and not to trust our own thought too much, or to get too wrapped up in solitary thinking. As individuals, we rebel at such advice, but most people are not individuals, and most individuals who disdain traditional wisdom are subject to fits of depression and ennui caused by a simple failure to practice good mental hygiene to avoid accidentally descending into chaotic thinking.

Understand that we are talking about circuits here, not thoughts, it's not the content of the loopback that is important ("It's God's will" is not exactly profound), but its capacity to drain off excess charge or excitement from a circuit. Loopbacks work at the circuit level, not the level of rational thought, they perform brain hygiene practices to keep the mind in balance.

Given that we have a structural need for loopbacks, does it matter where we get them from? It turns out that it does, and the reason it matters is because the purblind defect prevents us from seeing the circuits that our loopbacks create. That is, we think of a loopback as a saying, but the functional part of a loopback is the structure under the saying that connects into our cognitive circuitry. So, we reject traditional loopbacks because they are superstitions, or because God obviously doesn't exist, or because they are otherwise primitive and we're so sophisticated. This leads us to substitute more 'rational' apothegms that sound better to our ear without being able to see or understand the implications of the design of the circuitry hidden underneath the words. This can lead to disastrous results.

The modern secular university religion, for example, is based on righteousness, victimhood, and hatred of other, so instead of calming down our runaway circuits, woke sayings about punching fascists morph into vituperative asseverations that only true believers are in possession of absolute truth and moral goodness, and everyone else who disagrees with them should be reprogrammed, banished, or worse. In their ignorance and arrogance, these idiots that dominate universities today have supplanted traditional beliefs with their own enlightened dogma and ideology with the result that they have thrown away the progress of the last thousand years and replaced modern tolerance with secular religions that are on par with fourteenth century Christianity and Islam for narrow mindedness, intolerance, and bigotry.

The bottom line is that loopbacks should come from traditional, proven sources, instead of from the fevered minds of ideologues, because it's not the content that counts, but the circuit that it creates, and you're not smart enough to figure out what those are before your cute little sayings have begun to destroy lives. Glean the fields of traditional belief systems to find loopbacks that work for you, don't try to come up with your own. Pick ones that have passed the test of time for calming the mind down without inflaming the partisan passions of the group.[1]

---

[1]Ok, that sounds a lot like advice, but it's pretty generic and dictated by the lower level circuitry of the mind. Use it or not, it's a description of brain function, not an opinion on religion or philosophy.

Chapter 7

Alienation

A Stranger In A Strange Land

Feeling out of place, feeling kind of uncomfortable, feeling like something's a little off — we all go through this every now and again, some more often than others. Some of us get a touch of this almost everyday, while others just encounter it in certain difficult situations. We usually think that this out-of-kilter feeling is a small thing, like a ghost emotion that sneaks up on us and lurks around for a while.

Turns out, alienation — that's what this feeling is — is a much larger, much more important phenomenon than the well-balanced among us would ever suspect. But, those who are haunted by it daily know all too well that alienation can be a profound emotional force.

There are different kinds of alienation, but our focus here is on *informational* alienation because it arises from the structure of our mind by way of our individual choices. It is a very powerful type of alienation that we encounter daily, but know nothing about. We usually just chalk it up to mood, psychology, or situational difficulties. It occurs when our cognitive process eliminates chunks of our world from our mental purview by blacking out parts of problem spaces that show no sign of being either a threat or an opportunity. This action simplifies our mindscape and makes our reasoning process faster and more efficient. In its lightest form, informational alienation is just shorthand for saying 'don't bother to look here'.

Informational alienation is a way of mentally marking certain problem areas as spaces to be avoided that we don't need to waste any time investigating. `Avoid` is different both from `ignore` and `fear`, it's more of a shortcut than a warning, and all it costs us is a reduction in the scope of our world, and a reduction in the area in which we can use our abilities to solve our problems. You ignore for unimportance, you avoid for supposed efficiency, but you pay for it with lost opportunity.

The Structure of Alienation

We are going to use a structural, linguistic approach to examine alienation here, not a therapeutic one. We'll explore alienation by looking at the tendency of our mental machinery to generate feelings of alienation completely independent of a triggering event. Let me repeat that: we will look at how alienation can occur without a triggering event. If this approach holds up, it means that trying to treat some cases of alienation from a psychological perspective would be a misleading waste of time.

In order to better understand the place that alienation has in our reasoning and feelings, we need to learn about the language of feelings. This language comes from our model, and is based on testable mathematical relations instead of ideology or psychobabble. This will allow us to see how feelings from all intellect levels work together, and how we can use higher level ideas to understand the complexities of our weird L2 level mind. What we are looking for is a better way of understanding both our normal, as well as pathological, feelings, and normal, as well as philosophical, ideas.

Once we understand that alienation is part of the structure of evaluation-based cognition, we can begin to learn how to deal with it as an artifact of consciousness, instead of regarding it solely as a *true* feeling, a psychological state, or a perception of some external reality.

Language of Alienation

The vocabulary of alienation arises naturally from the evaluation structure of the mind, just like the words for positive and negative feelings do. It takes no imagination to understand that the a and p letters can represent the range of love and hate emotions, and the combination of the two can capture ambivalence. But, we've never previously acknowledged, or maybe even understood, that alienation is on the same level as love and hate. In this section, we will briefly introduce the language of alienation to demonstrate how naturally the more complex, three part emotional terms, which color so much of our experience, emerge from the model.

Alphabet of Feelings

In order to understand the language of feelings, we first have to understand how feelings naturally arise from the alphabet of evaluation that is built into our brain. The 3 letter alphabet of the evacule is:

> **a**: anti-self,
>
> **p**: pro-self,
>
> **n**: non-self;

which correlates to these obvious emotional counterparts:

> **a**: hate, fear
>
> **p**: love, need
>
> **n**: alienate, avoid

The value range for each of these dimensions of the evacule array will be from `minimum` to `maximum`. For simplicity's sake, we can analyze our problem with just the three values of `LOW, MED, HI`, but should the need ever arise, we could use numbers for greater precision, such as 0 to 10 or 0 to 100, etc.

Just think of [a,p,n] as the primary colors of emotion, like red, green, and blue are the primary colors of the spectrum. In the feeling spectrum, the pure value is set at MED, with HI being a more intense, and LO a less intense version of the MED value. This approach produces the following table of archetypes:

Scale	Anti-Self	Pro-Self	Non-self
HI	despise	adore	shun
MED	hate	love	disgust
LO	dislike	like	prohibited
Zero	—	—	—

The columns are a verbal representation of the values
HI, MED, LO, and 0, within the context of each header.
The entries are just meant to suggest levels of a type of
feeling, and can be altered as needed. The scale can be
reset, too, with the pure emotion being set to the HI value
instead of the MED value, if that makes more sense to you.

Vocabulary of Alienation

Let's see what happens when we define the vocabulary
of alienation in terms of the values in the evacule. We
will examine six alienation words: avoid, noxious, exclude,
yearn, dehumanize, and alienated.

Avoid

$$\textbf{avoid} : n = \texttt{LOW}$$

When your parents tell you to stay away from certain kids
because they are a bad influence, you can minimally reg-
ister that warning with a low n evaluation because you

don't always take your parents' warnings seriously. The n factor indicates a *not me, not my kind* type of evaluation, but the low level indicates that we aren't very invested in it. So, what does a low n evaluation accomplish? Not much, as it turns out, but it can represent the fact that rules that we don't think much of, are easy to violate. Higher n values are much more effective in enforcing the avoid rule.

Moral lessons often don't take — even though religious training tries to hammer home the message that named prohibitions should be assigned the highest n value possible — because learning the desired values depends on our cooperation to assign that value to the idea in our own mind. However, if the student is already alienated from the subject, or from their parent or teacher to begin with, then even the strongest warnings will likely only produce a low n that will have little effect on unsupervised behavior.

Avoid with the low n value is the simplest, least effective form of avoid, and as n gets ratcheted up it will have a stronger impact on behavior. At the moment, I find it hard to name an emotion to match [0, 0, MAX], because it seems more likely that the highest values of n would generally be matched with higher levels of a, since an urgency to avoid would likely entail some serious sense

of anti-self threat, but matching all values of the evacule
with emotion words is a task for another day.

Noxious

$$\textbf{noxious}: \text{n} \geq \text{MED} + \text{a} \geq \text{MED}$$

The two elements of **noxious** are present when the non-
self and anti-self values are both set at a MED or HI
evaluation. **Noxious** triggers feelings of revulsion, of dis-
gust, that are proportional to the level of a, and **avoid**
or **exclude** behavior proportional to the level of n. This
response is very useful in helping us to avoid bad food
and water, for example, but we can apply this feeling to
humans and our relations with them, as well, which can
cause all sorts of problems.

Exclude

$$\textbf{exclude}: \text{n} \geq \text{MED}, \text{ a,p} \leq \text{LOW}$$

Exclude means to fence something outside of the bounds
of consideration, it is the pure form of alienation. More
than just ignoring something, **exclude** means that we no
longer bother to investigate anything in a certain area.
This is a very powerful, world-limiting concept. For example, many students — to their detriment — **exclude**

mathematics from consideration for their area of study because it looks too hard.

Dehumanize

$$\textbf{dehumanize}: \texttt{a = HI, n = HI}$$

When we maximally alienate someone or something that we also hate, this gives us license to destroy it without compunction. High n gives us a free pass to do whatever we want without guilt because the object we despise shares none of our human rights or characteristics.

Yearn

Yearning, the great romantic emotion, can be represented by:

$$\textbf{yearn}: \texttt{n = LOW + p > LOW}$$

This defines an unfulfilled (and likely unexpressed) yearning as being a combination of a low level non-self evaluation that makes us feel that, for whatever reason, the object of our desire is beyond our reach, plus a significant pro-self evaluation that represents desire.

Alienated

$$\textbf{alienated}: \texttt{n} \geq \texttt{MED + a,p} \leq \texttt{MED}$$

When our positive/negative evaluation of something is MED or less — meaning that we don't really have a stake in it one way or the other — and we have assigned it a significant amount of n, this puts us into an alienated state, a state of disengagement that we have no motivation to overcome. In the evaluation process, the n dimension is the "I'm not involved" aspect in action. That is, alienation delineates a boundary between the part of our world we inhabit and the part occupied by a thing or things from which we have separated ourself.

We can evaluate something as **ignorable** just by setting both a and p to MIN without having to involve n, because attaching an alienation status to something takes independent effort that produces a result beyond just not caring about it. "It means nothing to me" is not the same thing as "that is totally *not* me". Assigning a high n is akin to ceding/alienating ground to a primordial otherness we refuse to acknowledge or to engage with. We choose to alienate things when our sense of strength, vitality, or interest is so low in relation to something that to pay attention to it would deprive us of the ability to attend to other things that we know are more important, which includes doing or thinking nothing.

Ubiquity of Alienation

Far from being a modern personality affliction, alienation is so fundamental to our mental structure that it is one of the big three attributes in the evaluation atom, the evacule, the n in $[a,p,n]$. This inherited structure, the core of all of our thinking, upon which our entire mind is built, only has a finite number of ways to encode emotions, and about 50% of them involve a significant amount of alienation mixed in with positive and negative feelings. This means that in the full spectrum of evaluations that our mind can make, only 50% of them do *not* include a moderate to high dose of alienation.

The good news is that this in no way implies that 1/2 of our emotions or thoughts must involve alienation, just that half of the words in our evaluation/emotional vocabulary do involve it. Feeling alienated comes from alienating too much of your world when you evaluate it. The more you alienate, the less interested, curious and engaged you will feel, and this corresponds to a higher degree of alienation in general.

Evaluating something as uninteresting suffices to dismiss it. Alienating inaccessible or sterile parts of your world can optimize information processing, but using alienation as a psychological crutch to shore up an underdeveloped, inadequate personality leads to feelings of isolation and hopelessness, and makes one vulnerable to the siren call of cults.

Informational alienation can manifest as psychological, or even social alienation when used in excess. The world can be an open and potentially interesting place when we approach it with an open and curious attitude, but once we have deliberately alienated too much of it, rather than seeing the world as an integrated whole with both risk and opportunity, it begins to look like a number of small oases of safety and acceptance among large, forbidding areas of off-limits darkness. Then, rather than being a wonderland for exploration and discovery, the world becomes a dangerous jungle of hazards and areas not meant for us.

The essence of cultism is the decision to alienate otherness, not just others, but all others who are unlike you, who are not part of your immediate group. The decision to do this is strictly a move in group dynamics to separate and grow the group by isolating members from other groups and making them 100% dependent on this group. There is no doctrine involved, the claim that there is, is just window dressing meant to make it look like this pure power move has a higher purpose.

When taken to extremes, we can wind up alienating so

much of our internal and external reality that we gut our world of substance, meaning, and potential. Informational alienation ranges from being a little mark on a map, to being the debilitating mental and social illness that began as an infection in the university, but has recently broken out into the body politic by burning through the thin wall of the post-adolescent generation.

If we don't watch our step, if we fail to follow good mental hygiene practices, we could find our life story inadvertently being written in the jargon of alienation. So, just as some of us swear in almost every sentence we utter, and some of us never swear at all, it's ultimately up to us to decide how much of our experience we want to interpret with our alienation vocabulary.

The critical point to understand about our emotional palette is that alienation is an efficiency mutation that allows us to partition our mental world into knowable and unknowable regions. The benefit of doing this is that we get to focus our attention on high value targets and ignore dead ends. That is, since our cognition is evaluation based, rather than knowledge based, then it makes sense that the ability to dismiss entire regions of the mindscape would be a very useful optimization since, once we have evaluated a region as sterile and useless, or even just high risk and low reward, then repeating the evaluation every time we scan the area would just be a pointless waste of time and effort.

The problem of alienation as a personality disorder arises when the developmental stage of adolescence fails to produce an independent, self-actuated adult, and allows a timorous, dependent child to emerge, unprepared, into the overwhelming world of adult responsibilities. Such a superannuated child will resort to using informational alienation to block out threatening or demanding parts of his world to cocoon himself in the safety of an unending childhood sanctioned by overindulgent caretakers, a cult, or a cult-like ideology.

The significance of this is that the uncomfortable emotional state we associate with alienation is produced by the exclusionary **avoid** decision and action, i.e., the *feelings* of alienation are the emotional side effect of misusing a cognitive simplification function as a psychological crutch. The feelings are a consequence, not a cause, and their intensity is entirely defined by the intensity of the revulsion we accept when we are doing the evaluation. The more we pepper our evaluations with gratuitous levels of high n, the more problems we will experience with emotional alienation.[1]

We think that alienation reflects on the worth of things in reality, but that's just because we mistakenly think that our word-based mind is the center and true judge of all things real. Frequent high n evaluations are a product of our choice, of our desire to keep the challenging world at bay, of our unwillingness to engage with experience. It's like we choose to paint our room in a hideous color and then bemoan the ugliness of our daily life. Aware or not, we choose our path.

There are other kinds of alienation, including psychological or solitary alienation, and social or collective alienation.

Psychological alienation is an affliction of affluence and leisure because together they allow narcissism to bloom into a toxic level of disrespect and disdain for all who do not serve the narcissist's personal needs. In its most extreme form, alienation is a bitch, a nasty, gnawing fungus in our brain that tells us that nothing is worth anything, that we are utterly alone and isolated from everything good and worthwhile, or it can even tell us that nothing is good and worthwhile. At its darkest depths, we can even become alienated from ourself, from our own thoughts and

---

[1] *"Keep on the sunny side of life"* is a loopback that helps some avoid excessive alienation evaluations.

feelings, from our potential to achieve something and to become what we might be. In the extreme, we can even become alienated from life itself.

When widespread affluence develops in successful societies, ironically, psychological alienation can become a disease of society, with the most privileged and least challenged being the most vulnerable to it. When the literati adopt alienation as a style, they can spread it throughout society like the most deadly contagious disease.

In the current day, social alienation is such a problem that entire departments in universities exist for no other reason than to spread alienation and a righteous sense of victimhood to as many people as possible. Humanities faculties are teaching — in required courses, no less — that the only way forward is by dismantling science, mathematics, engineering, and everything else that works in society and the economy, so that it can be replaced by a vengeful, implacable tyranny of the one right truth (which, to no one's surprise, turns out to be theirs).

Affluence and public support for the arts and higher education in the humanities make a deadly mixture, because it tends to groom under-performing narcissists, known as graduates, to be super spreaders of alienation.

Conclusion

The point is that feelings of alienation are not actually caused by external events, they are potholes built into our consciousness into which we can fall with an unwary step. That is, it is false to claim that event x caused us to feel alienated, because the process is that our evaluation of x assigned it an n value that the emotional part of our mind can experience as alienation. Nothing in reality can force a particular evaluation.

We feel alienation because we invite it, or fail to avoid it, not because it is an accurate description of the events in our life. It is possible to evaluate disappointing events and outcomes appropriately without veering into the wasteland of alienation. By a quirk of evolution, our mental structures are flawed in the sense that we have much more capacity to feel alienation than can be justified by anything in physical reality, and even more than is needed to describe the complexities of semantic reality.

One has to wonder if alienation is an adaptation that allows the lower levels of group hierarchies to quietly resign themselves to their limited opportunities, and to accept, however reluctantly, whatever share of the pie they can get.

Strategic use of informational alienation can be a tool

of good information flow management, and judicious alienation of avoidable areas won't make you feel bad or miss much that is of value. However, there are two different ways to misuse this type of alienation: 1) alienate too much, and 2) alienate unavoidable things.

Humanities students often alienate too much of their world, rejecting the concept of rigor as being unduly confining of their inner genius, their higher spirit's freedom of creativity and invention. When this leads to the rejection of mathematics, science, computing, and engineering not only from their curriculum, but from their sphere of interest, as well, they are rejecting even the possibility of learning anything about objective reality. While they may prosper despite this choice, they are forfeiting the possibility of ever participating in any discussions of anything higher than self-interest and group supremacy.

Alienating the unavoidable, such as things you encounter regularly — be it math, an idea, or a person — can color your experience of life by exposing you to routine encounters with the dread of peering into the abyss, and generally making you feel smaller in relation to the challenges of life.

Since alienation is a core function of the mind, it cannot be eliminated or avoided, nor can there can be one correct way to handle it. It does not even make sense to consider it a bad thing that must be fixed. I mean, you can die from drinking too much water, but that doesn't mean you should cut it out of your life, you just need to know how to manage your use of the resource properly. Similarly, sometimes alienation is a good thing, but when we overindulge ourselves in it, it can damage or end our lives, just like any overindulgence can. When we build a political movement around it, it can become a true source of evil.

The ubiquity of alienation in one's world correlates highly with a failure to mature into a competent, independent adult. Stunted post-adolescents feel that, by themselves, they are trapped and powerless against the forces that shape and control their world, so they eagerly seek groups that promise recognition, protection, and power in exchange for submission.

Alienation, when raised to the level of a creed, generates powerful and dangerous ideologies because it attracts adherents with the seductive pitch that **we**, the special, the educated, the enlightened few, are morally superior to the uninitiated, the great unwashed. Collectivist cults teach that the only reason that **we** have nothing and **they** have everything is because the world is unjust, and the nasty oppressors will keep everything to themselves that we should all share equally. The only solution to this injustice, they say, is for **us** to take everything from **them**, the people who are in no way like us.

Surely, learning about how our mind actually works, and what the function of alienation is, and what its attendant risks are, will put us in a better position to manage alienation by enhancing our abilities to successfully engage with the challenges of life.

The alienation dimension of the evacule is not really any more toxic than the other two dimensions. After all, overusing either of them is just as dangerous as overusing alienation: evaluating everything as evil would leave you alone with nothing to eat or drink, and evaluating everything as sunshine and lollipops could get you killed in a day.

Learning how to be comfortable and competent when engaging with the unknown, both psychologically and intellectually, can make a significant difference with how large, or shrunken, we allow our world of opportunity to become. That is, because proficiency in the art of L3 querying demands maximal use of all of our intellectual resources, working towards that level of intellectual competence tends to generate a very useful immunity to alienation.

Chapter 8

Values & Warped Space

We need to grok that our mind natively sees reality through a value lens before we can understand how our values and morals really work. Our ability to evaluate, to place a value on things we perceive, precedes and underlies our ability to think.

The harsh news is that natural selection wiped out the parts of the population that didn't share the core values that became the archetypes that drive our instinctual behaviors. That is, our values depend on our genetically encoded mortality interests. How could they not? We are living, reproducing life forms with a bias towards life, and more specifically, a profound bias towards our own successful life. Our core values are based on our mortality interests: what's good for our survival is good, what threatens us is bad, and what has no effect is unimportant.

Your initial response to the idea that all of our values are based on self-interest might be to protest that our behavior is also, or primarily, driven by higher religious and moral ideals. You may object that self-interest is too base, too selfish, too small to account for our tendency to sacrifice ourselves for family and country. That would be true if our mind worked the way we think it does, but it doesn't, and that's why most of our ideas about morality and ideals are just plain wrong.

It's not that our moral values themselves are wrong, or that others are right, it's just that we're wrong about how our mind produces the results we see. That's why we are so often surprised and disappointed, both by ourselves and our fellow humans, when we regularly fall short of our ideals. We're routinely surprised when people in our circle succumb to the pleasures of the flesh. But, we should ask ourselves, what is surprising about people being driven to behaviors — such as promiscuous sex, intoxication, and gambling — that directly trigger intense pleasure centers in their brain? Yes, we know that there is potentially a steep price to be paid for making this choice, but we also have to admit that temptation often overwhelms caution when the reward is a thrill that resonates with our life needs and force.

The traditional response to moral failures is to exhort the lost souls to heed the preaching of morality and ethics from whatever authority they accept. Obviously, this only works in a small number of cases for a short period of time, while most sinners just continue in sin. The problem is that, while the message may be right, the mechanism of reasoning and behavioral control doesn't work anything at all like we think it does, so when we try to guide our behavior with the controls that we know about, we often just wind up hitting another wall.

Take weight control for a prosaic example. Of course, the bottom line is that we gain weight if caloric intake exceeds caloric expenditure, but that doesn't mean you can control your intake by counting calories. Why not? Well, we have decades of evidence that nearly everyone with a weight problem who tries this solution fails, and whether or not we can explain why it fails, we have to deal with the fact that it does.

The routine, even predictable, failure of inculcated morality and calorie restriction to achieve their stated goals in a significant percentage of the population should give us a clue that there must be something we don't understand. So, even if you, personally, are never tempted, and never overindulge, that still doesn't overcome the mountain of evidence that these old saws do not successfully solve these problems for most people.

We cannot understand morality until we understand that the self has an expandable border that separates *that which must be defended* from everything else. What we think of as our self concept didn't come into being until well after verbal language came on the stage, and our focus here is on the much earlier, more elemental, pre-verbal self. The concept of the `self` and what we understand with the pronouns `I` and `we` are not at all the same thing. `I` is in the specific, or lesser self, while `we` is in the extended, or greater, self that includes the lesser or specific self.

Before animals could develop the ability to maintain stable hierarchical groups, or even to care for their offspring, they had to have developed the ability to extend their idea of the self — the *that* which must be protected — to include others, to a greater or lesser degree, such as family, unit, or clan. This means that we will sometimes sacrifice our own bodies to save the greater self, of which we now consider ourselves a part. Our values, though, remain unchanged, it's just that the *boundary* of the self that we are protecting has been stretched far enough so that we can willingly die to save the part of our greater self that doesn't include us.

Once our ability to expand our concept of the self, our concept of what has to be saved, becomes flexible, then it can expand and contract to include or exclude others. You can see good examples of this in the animal kingdom if you study bears or other generally solitary animals, for example. The mother's sense of self expands to include her cubs, whom she will protect from their father as well as all other threats. Yet, at the end of their adolescence, she will shrink her sense of self again, and chase her offspring away to start their own independent lives, so that she can shift her focus to raising the next generation.

Thus, a genetically defined self-interest-based value system is perfectly consistent with ideals such as heroism and self-sacrifice. Please note that this is consistent with other evolved abilities that extend an existing ability into a new ability by only changing one small detail instead of an entire complex of behaviors. In this case, it is the ability to expand the sense of self, which suddenly makes it possible for previously solitary creatures to become co-operative and sociable.

The significance of the fact that `value` springs from our mental conception of our own mortality interests, is that the world has to look different to each and every one of us, because we are interpreting it from the point of view of our temporal needs and resources. We don't see things as they are, we see them through the lens of evaluation from the perspective of self-interest. This is not a shortcoming on our part that we can overcome, this is how the equipment is built, and it cannot be changed, nor should it be.

Because our cognition is evaluation-based, not knowledge-based, our values warp our perceptual sphere to prize or fear things increasingly as they approach the center of our mortality interest. We don't perceive the world from a neutral point of view, we always understand reality from our own warped space inside of our own head, instead of from a neutral position.

In other words, things you see in your side view mirror appear closer than they actually are. Our perception is distorted by our need to react quickly enough to survive, so both threats and opportunities are magnified non-linearly as they approach us. Intellectually, we know that a lion is a lion just the same whether it's 10 feet away, or a mile away, but since its threat to us increases disproportionately as its distance from us decreases, our value system bends our perception in such a way that the importance of things 10 feet away is maybe 1,000 or 10,000 times greater than it would be when the object is 100 feet away.

Even though we may belong to a religion that we take very seriously, and even though we might sacrifice ourselves for the group or its ideals, our value judgments still come from our center, a private place where our evaluation of our needs and resources gets turned into a movement solution to the latest crisis.

The very nature of a personal space — the perceptual sphere that defines our view of the world — is that it is warped by our values, because things get more important the closer they are to our greater self, and less important the further away they are, regardless of their inherent, observable impact on the lives or fortunes of the community they directly impact. This does not mean that we are selfish or bad, just that we are mortal beings who can instantly die the moment we skip a beat in the ongoing struggle for life.

It's neither a good, nor a bad thing that our view of the world is warped by our evaluation of it, it simply is, exactly like gravity just is. The warpage of perception only becomes a problem when, through the action of the purblind defect, we fail to see it. Those of us who wear corrective lenses know that our eyesight is bad, so we compensate for it. Just so, I'm not saying that we're supposed to give up our warped view of the world, just that we should know about it so that we can learn to use tools that allow us to see the world from other, different perspectives, too, in case the time comes when being able to do so would prove useful.

Meaning

Meaning, as in, "What's the meaning of life?" is different than value. Evaluation is a primordial process that produces a visceral feeling of right and wrong, good and bad, truth and lie, friend and enemy, threat and opportunity, importance and triviality. We can feel the difference between friend and foe, we can feel truth in our breast, we can feel enraged when we are wronged. Although evaluation can involve words and word ideas, underneath it all, evaluation is a pre-verbal process that translates perceptions into our own personal language that defines degrees of right and wrong, and good and bad that can be translated directly into action.

Meaning, in contrast, is based on word ideas that we learn from our social contacts throughout our lives. Meaning connects our individual life struggles to a greater world, either to that of a group or society, or to a civilization through important ideas we derive from it.

The nature of meaning is such that if you fail to define meaning in your own life, then your own life truly does become meaningless, but this has nothing to do with whether or not someone else's life has meaning, or whether yours could have it if you were willing to do the work. The funny thing is that ideologues with advanced degrees sagely tell us that there is no meaning in a reality that doesn't support or allow meaning, yet they fail to even look for it in the reality that both creates and supports it.

Meaning can be found either in a group, or in an abstraction. When we find our meaning in a group, we expose ourself to the risk of becoming narrow minded and intolerant of anyone outside of the group, and we become vulnerable to being sucked into a cult. Groups just embody the ambition of the leader, so the meaning that his/her group offers is just an extension of their values with all their strengths and shortcomings.

Joining a group with a long established record of supporting positive, productive societies, like some religions, can reduce the risk of cultism somewhat. A problem with cultism can arise whenever the only two points on our value-meaning line are our internal values and the values of our group's leader. In that case, then we are still living in a world of maximum warpage where all of our perceptions are strongly distorted by one narrow set of moral truths that are suspiciously similar to blind self-interest.

The alternative to the two point value line is the three point value line that we can define for ourselves when we add a serious definition of the ultimate as the endpoint to the line that connects the self to the group. Defining the ultimate should only include concepts of the unattainable ideal, and exclude temporal notions such as power. This is the only way to place the ideal of the ultimate above and separate from the needs of the group. The benefit of the third point is that it gives us a position from which we can critique how well the group's ideas are in line with our ideals of the ultimate.

Where do we get the the definition of the ultimate? One example is provided to us in the very name, *Israel,* which literally means *god wrestler.* The concept of god wrestling is that by staying in faith while avoiding piety, and refusing to blindly follow authority, we can step up and accept our personal responsibility to interrogate the ultimate directly, instead of through an intermediary. How do we equip ourselves for such a humongous responsibility? Well, it ain't easy, but the beginning of the road is to be found in the ground between piety and cynicism, which, you must admit, leaves us a very large area to begin our work in.

Conclusion

Do people in a group tend to share values, or at least to claim to do so? Of course, but this is just the mechanism of the greater, or extended, self at work. Groups whose members share no higher values have no coherence and simply fade away. If you go to the park on a weekend and wind up playing a team sport with strangers, you have formed a temporary group with whom you only share the values of good sportsmanship, at best. The life expectancy of that kind of group is generally measured in minutes or hours.

The key to understanding how values work, and where they come from, is to grasp that the self is flexible, not fixed. It can expand and contract in different conditions to include or exclude others, to create a greater self, or to shrink to just include our own being. Once you can see groups as an extension of the self, rather than the self as a member of the group, then you can begin to understand both the power and the weakness of groups. Groups do not actually exist independently of the voluntary cooperation of their key members. If a group, for whatever reason, stops providing its members with what they need, then the membership will just start to evaporate, and the group will wither away, revealing that it was never the source of its own power.

As we begin to understand our relation to groups, we should be able to see that group dynamics doesn't change the fact that the calculus of `value` is centered in our mortality interests. The purblind defect makes it difficult for us to see how we are only attached to our favorite groups by an *internal* link, a link that exists only inside of us. What we think of as higher, selfless feelings are just selfish mortality interests transposed to the setting of the greater self, and what is really happening is that we bring others under the umbrella of our own self-interest, not that we abjure our own self interest in favor of the interests of others.

When we join a group like a religion of a political movement, we connect our internal values with the group creed. If we have character, we can only do this if we can see their belief system as being an extension of our own, as being a means to empower us to be productive in ways that are beyond anything we can achieve on our own. When we join, or align ourself with a group, we are including the group in our greater self. Whenever we combine the larger with the smaller, the center of gravity shifts towards the center of the larger, except, in this case, it's the center of the self that shifts and extends our concept of our self-interest towards the group center.

Why can groups that claim a higher purpose so routinely commit such terrible crimes against humanity with such impunity as they undeniably do? It's because the group's purpose is really just amplified self-interest, not some higher ideal, and this is precisely why we have to define our own three point line to avoid falling into supporting group tyranny.

Chapter 9

Opinions

Opinions are not what you think they are, and they do not do what you think they do.

You think that opinions are a product of reasoning — and up to a point, some of them are — and you think that they play a part in reasoning, but that is something which they certainly do not do, something they cannot do, something that they are neither designed nor equipped to do. They're actually built to do kind of the opposite of reasoning.

Stop! Before you reject this idea outright, allow the time needed for a reflective pause to get you into the frame of mind where you can disinterestedly consider a spectrum of possibilities, including the possibility that I might be right about this. If you think about it, it would explain a

Opinion Object
conclusion/statement
truth value
group links
opinion links
true bucket
false bucket

Table 9.1: Opinion Data Object

lot, wouldn't it? I mean if opinions were actually obstacles to reasoning, instead of tools to help reasoning? Wouldn't that explain the futility of debate?

The very structure of an opinion makes it completely impossible for it to be used as part of any actual reasoning process. Yes, you can use opinions in arguments and discussions, but arguments and discussions are social interactions, they are not reasoning exercises. Never have been, never will be.

The reason that opinions don't behave like we expect them to, is because they are not built that way (notice a theme here?). Table 9.1 shows a model of the opinion object that actually behaves exactly the way opinions do in real life. Let's walk through it element by element.

1. The `conclusion/statement` is the idea content of the opinion, the assertion that x is y, or whatever. There is no constraint on what this element can be,

and no requirement that it make any sense whatso-ever. When we build an opinion by ourself, this is the conclusion that we think comes from our reading of the data.

2. The `truth value` is whatever degree of truth we assign to the statement, it is a measure of how passionate we are about the idea.

3. The `group links` are the critical element in the opinion, because opinions are a unit of exchange that we use to cement or improve our position in various groups. When we take on a new opinion in the process of joining a group, it is permanently bound to that group.

4. The `opinion links` are important because all of our opinions, without exception, are connected to some or all of our other opinions. It is these links between opinions that form the web of beliefs and feelings that define our world view.

5. The `true bucket` is where we link messages, ideas, or opinions that are consistent with this opinion.

6. The `false bucket` is where we link messages, ideas, or opinions that contradict or disagree with this opinion.

There are two ways to create an opinion object. The

first way is to sort through some related ideas, and divide them into true and false buckets according to some rule or conclusion that you have come to. Then, whenever you decide just how true this opinion is — which can change repeatedly over time — you update the truth value field. The second, and more common way to create an opinion, is just to accept it from one of your groups, or from a group that you aspire to join.

Whatever its origin, you eventually link new opinions to each of your groups that you are sure will agree with it, as well as linking them to other related opinions you have in your web of ideas.

Once this is all done — and it all usually happens automatically, without you having to do anything deliberately — the opinion is ready to be used, it's ready to do its job, and you are now equipped to instantly have an opinion on any statement related to this topic, without having to do any more work. So, whenever a new written or verbal message comes in that relates to this topic, your mind will compare the content of the new message to this opinion's statement, and if it matches pretty well, it will be put into the *true*, supporting data, bucket. Otherwise, if it contradicts the statement in this opinion, it will be put into the false, contradicting data, bucket.

The job of an opinion is to be a static filter that helps us to manage the flow of incoming information. Opinions are static in the sense that, with the exception of the truth value, they are essentially immutable. They can be superseded by a new opinion, or the truth value can be changed, but the original opinion hangs around indefinitely.

Opinions are filters that sort incoming ideas into **good/true** and **bad/false** buckets. They are dumb filters in that they don't support any calculations. They just do a simple comparison of the incoming message to the opinion's statement/conclusion to determine its truth value.

We use opinions both to stay in sync with a linked group, and to maintain our personal equilibrium in our world as we see it. We use opinions to decide whether things we read and hear are right or wrong, so that we can immediately tag them accordingly. The advantage to this approach to dealing with information is that we can process new input almost instantaneously by using a simple comparison, without having to do any reasoning whatsoever, because we already know the answer before the question is asked.

The reason it is so hard to change someone's opinion is because changing an opinion is not just changing an idea, it involves changing one's group affiliations, social position, and sense of self as well, because changing an opinion breaks the links that connect us to all of the groups in our greater self, as well as those links that tied this opinion to everything else we thought we knew.

The `opinion`, you see, is not an intellectual construct. At its heart, an opinion is a sorting routine that is designed solely to maintain our mental and social equilibrium. We think that opinions are well thought out ideas that are supported by strong evidence, but this ignores the fact that opinions exist to process statements that are built entirely of words.

Wait, what? What else would opinions be made of, and deal with, if not words? Well, it turns out that words are complicated little buggers that are also not what we think they are. Words are covered in depth in the **Language** chapter. For now, we'll just point out that our assumption that words exist to transparently describe reality is wrong. This mistaken idea comes from our misapprehension that the center of our consciousness is in the part of our brain that thinks in word ideas, when the actual center of it is in the evolutionary seed from which it developed.

The fact is that words aren't normal, words aren't natural, words don't even have any meaning in physical reality. Words only exist *as* words, as semantic units, as anything other than sound, in semantic reality, and in our own personal pseudo-reality, the cognitive space inside of our head, where they function primarily as links to social groups, and only secondarily as the building blocks of ideas.

It's an illusion that words in informal languages describe reality, because the meaning of informal languages, particularly when referring to abstractions, cannot be verified within an acceptable margin of error. Only formal languages have that power and that precision.

If that is the case, then what purpose do words in natural languages serve? They serve to align us with our linked groups, and to allow us to interact with each other more or less well when dealing with physical objects that can be denoted with unambiguous signs and gestures. After all, if words had the capacity to communicate ideas, then how do you explain that I can tell you about a true idea only to have you disagree with it? The reason this happens all the time is because it's not possible to communicate precisely that part of an idea that makes it undeniably true to us, because that part is the personal value we place on its links to our groups and other ideas. It's not the content of the opinion that is true so much as it is the position that the opinion fills in our web of opinions and associations.

Yet, we continue on, using words to communicate ideas without noticing that we are using forks to scoop up water. "Well," you might ask, "what about the words I am reading in this paragraph, this book? Are we not repeating this same feckless charade?" Yes, we are, but with the small difference that the formal description of all of these ideas we are discussing is readily available in several highly technical volumes that spell out the whole model of the mind in formal language that can be coded up and tested. The words presented here are only meant to stimulate a feeling of curiosity about possibilities, and to trigger in you a germ of dissatisfaction with the traditional, primitive mode of thought that has trapped humanity in what has been an inescapable swamp in which progress in subjective matters has always been impossible.

Opinions are a filter that is built of words to sort messages made of words, they are not a component of rational argument. They are true because we deem them to be. We often do not agree on the truth of opinions because we are all using our own perception of reality to define that truth, perceptions that are beneficially distorted by our own needs and self-interest. The goal we have in creating opinions is to situate ourselves in a particular semantic reality context in the strongest position possible. This involves both being oriented to the implications of the message, and making sure that our evaluation of it agrees with what our nearest, most important groups would think of it.

Chapter 10

Predictions

What we think of as our higher intellect, our rational mind, the part of our brain that does word-based reasoning, that pretends to be all educated and logical and rational, that we think is our real, true, inner self, that we use to predict and plan the future, well, it's not exactly all that's it's cracked up to be.

How do you think that cells and structures in organic entities manage to do the level of thinking required to anticipate the future? Do you think that they somehow consume and comprehend all available data, then run numerous simulations to come up with a logical conclusion of the likelihood of particular future events? Yeah, right. No, that's not how the mind works.

But, media pundits want us to believe that their deep

knowledge of some sliver of the present endows them with the ability to foretell the future. We are awash in a polluted sea of incompetent predictions that are mostly wrong, yet no one is ever called to task for their failure to understand the present, let alone to predict the future accurately. It seems that the only way media types can respond to their false predictions is to make new, even more ridiculous ones. Yet, many of us tune into the clown show of the nightly news, faithfully, day in and day out.

Why do we listen to such tripe? The answer is simple: predicting the future is what L2 does, so on a subliminal level we find it reassuring that everyone else also expects the future to arise from the present as predictably as night follows day. But it seems to have escaped everyone's notice that this only happens within very short time frames, but over longer time frames, the future is always a product of some out-of-stream phenomenon unexpectedly colliding with the present to knock our world off of its axis.

The L2 mind endowed us with the ability to make situational predictions, to give us an early warning of what might be lurking behind that hill. It also gave us the ability to form larger and more complex social structures. Together, these new capabilities eventually enabled humans to become the most successful species in the history of this planet.

But, as always, there are unanticipated consequences, and in this case, the primary one was that the complexity of the reality of ideas and relationships soon overwhelmed the simplicity of physical reality. Most of the significant events that impact our lives and change our futures now come from semantic, not physical reality, and our ability to make short term predictions in physical reality does not apply to the complexity of semantic reality. The significance of this is that L2 evolved before semantic reality could begin to become complex, so it never had the opportunity to include any functionality capable of higher level reasoning in abstract reality. Our ability to predict the future is limited to whatever the pattern object can do, and this does not include the ability to predict the future in semantic reality. It does not include the ability to make strategic predictions at all.

In order to explain all of this, let's take a short stroll through the mind to look at how the different layers use their different inherited data objects to do their jobs. This will let us see how our mental capacity started with the ability to react to the present, then added the ability to learn from the past, and finally, built onto that foundation some kind of ability to anticipate the future, which we

Result Object
starting situation
action
ending situation
evaluation

Table 10.1: Result Data Object

mistake for the ability to make predictions.

L0, the first layer of the mind, just evaluates external senses down into an evacule, and combines that with an evaluation of internal state to come up with an action command that the body can implement. **Approach, retreat, ignore**: pretty basic stuff, but it makes for a model that does a very good job of explaining and predicting the basic behavior of the simplest volitionally mobile life forms.

L1 adds both memory and a structure to L0. The structure organizes our experience into a unit that can be evaluated, remembered, and recalled. This L1 combination of elements makes it possible for us to learn from experience.

The L1 structure is called the **result** object, and is shown in table 10.1. The **starting situation** is the collection of perceptions, ideas, and feelings in our current memory at the moment that we decided we had to react. A **situation** is the memorized version of current memory.

We can fine tune a `situation`'s contents later, as we see fit, since we retain it in memory, while current memory obviously just keeps changing.

So, when we are confronted with a new `situation` that we have to react to, we evaluate it, check our memory, and decide on an `action`. Afterwards, we look at the `ending situation`, which is what our `action` led to, and compare it to the `starting situation` to judge whether our life was improved, damaged, or unchanged by our action. Our assessment of the change goes into the evaluation field.

From then on, whenever we encounter a new `situation`, we go through our L1 memory to check whether we have ever seen anything like this before. If we have, we look at the evaluation in that memory to see if it's positive. If so, then we know that we can immediately take the same action as before, but if it's negative, then we have to take the time to come up with a new action.

So, the L1 `result` object is really simple, but still powerful enough to enable us to learn from experience, which, you must admit, is a huge advantage in the struggle for life. L1 abilities enable us to improve our choices as we age, with the result that, up to some point, what age takes away from us in strength and energy, L1 gives back to us in wisdom.

Take a moment and reflect on how much benefit we get from such a simple mutation that enables us to associate an evaluation with an action and an initial situation. The ability to learn from experience is a crucial skill for long term survival. So, given just how easily learning from experience can be implemented in an evolved mind, what do we expect the L2 `pattern` object — the structure that we use to anticipate the future — to look like? Shouldn't it also be kind of simple, maybe just a step or so above the `result` object? The answer is, yes, the `pattern` object is a lot like the `result` object, just enhanced a mite. But, it's certainly not some huge, complex computational structure that can divine the future by peering deeply into the realm of possibilities.

Where the `result` object has an `action` and a before and after `situation`, the `pattern` object has a before `situation`, an `action`, and up to a half dozen or so different `next step` options, which are just more linked patterns. It's the next step options, which we program into the pattern object ourselves, and an element that is not even in the object, that makes the `pattern` object so powerful and yet so limited.

The multiple next step options enable us to specify different paths to follow depending on how the last action turned out. While the `result` object just stores and scores the result of doing a particular action in a given situation, the pattern object stores different responses that we have devised over time, so that we have different possible responses to any number of situations that might result from an action.

If you imagine plotting out grammar rules, such as declensions and conjugations, in a branching form, you can see how talking about one male or one female would lead you down different branches of the tree to structure your sentences. This is the kind of thing that the pattern object natively supports.

However, the most significant way that the pattern object changed the way we think is that it forces us to see the world in terms of patterns: v follows u, w leads to x, y, z. The pattern object *patternizes* our thought process, it changes our cognitive system from reactive to expectant/proactive. Whereas L0 and L1 creatures react to events, L2 creatures look at the world expecting to see patterns, relations, cause and effect. This predilection to see relations among things we observe is built into our reasoning by the structural bias of the pattern object.

Being able to understand that an experience is a one-off, and not part of a pattern, is actually a strain for the L2

Pattern Object	Possible Next Step
evaluation starting situation action	
	option 1, best case option 2, next best option 3, next best option 4, middle case option 5, next worst option 6, next worst option 7, worst case

Table 10.2: Pattern Object

mind, so much so that a lot of our thinking throughout the day is spent trying to make random events fit into a larger scheme so that they make more sense to us. It's as though, because L2 is built to organize relations and sequences, it is confused by the meaningless and unpredictable.

The pattern object natively supports the path structure, a sequence of contingent steps that leads to a goal, as well as a plan structure that incorporates numerous paths to support complex, long term planning.

In a brilliant example of elegant design, the pattern object gains most of its functionality without having to add any additional structure whatsoever. The L2 `compare` function that works on the pattern object identifies the best next step by using `current memory` as a parameter, and comparing it to each of the next step options we built into the pattern in order to identify which branch to continue on.

So, L2 works a plan by taking whatever is in `current memory` that demands attention, finding a `pattern` with a matching `starting situation`, then performing the `action` in it to start the plan. L2 then works the plan to completion by comparing what's in current memory after an action to the `starting situation` in each of the available next step options, and repeating that for each step in the process. This is how it figures out which step to take next until the task completes, after which our mind just returns to its default `scan` and `seek` mode.

This all works because pattern objects can be chained to each other with virtual, conditional branches that the `compare` function evaluates. This is why it can support path constructs with a sequence of contingent steps, and this is what enables us to do multi-step tasks. We use the pattern object to build paths to get from situation *a* to situation *b* all day, everyday, in almost everything we do, from work tasks, to driving, to planning our day, to communicating with language. As a practical matter, the pattern object is the basis of all human and advanced animal societies.

But, it is only after we add language, and word-based

ideas and reasoning to the mix that things get really interesting, because it is at this point that the cognitive organism achieves the ability to think in abstractions and to be aware of itself (the self is an abstraction of the totality of one's functions). Apparently, as soon as we could handle abstract thought, someone, or many individuals, at more or less the same time, figured out that the pattern object has a really cool power: it lets us imagine the future.

Here's the elegant optimization that makes that possible: when we use a path construct that defines a plan, we don't actually have to do the prescribed actions. What does a plan buy us when we don't actually follow it? It gives us the opportunity to play out the plan in the abstract world of our thought, instead of in the reality of the physical world. This should sound familiar, because we all do this everyday, naturally, without even thinking about it, or having been trained in it.

We can explore options to known plans by asking ourself, "What happens if I do step 1, but then, rather than taking the *option 1* next step, I take the *option 4* next step, or even try a novel step that's never been done before?"

Our ability to anticipate the future comes directly from our ability *to think through* the steps of pattern sequences, instead of *acting* on each step. By imagining, instead of actually taking, actions, we are, in effect, projecting the past into the future, but we are doing this with a degree of freedom that allows us to see futures that transcend experience and only exist in our imagination. The question then becomes, can we make any of these futures happen?

This ability to plan an anticipated future is exactly the same thing as our ability to predict the future, except that in the planning case we try to make it happen, and in the predicting case we are just the observer. The impetus behind our various imaginings of different futures is sometimes based partly on experience, partly on learned patterns, but mostly on our emotional state, our mood, our attitude, our hopes, dreams, needs, and fears. The stronger and more powerful our feelings in a particular situation are, the more likely we are to make plans. The weaker and more impotent we feel, the more likely we are to predict futures happening to us.

What is the result? What kind of predictions do we come up with? Mostly, we come up with a scenario of a future that seems plausible or certain *to us*. Nothing more. Will some of these predictions come true? Undoubtedly, yes, but how many? 1%, 50%, 95%? My guess is that the success rate would be in the lower end of that range, but I also suspect that most people would differ vigorously with that, and claim that their prediction accuracy is in the higher end of the range. But, if we are honest with ourselves, deep down, we know that we only get away with claiming that most of our predictions are right because we don't keep records of every prediction, and because we are more likely to remember our correct predictions than our incorrect ones.

There are two obvious problems with this anticipation process: 1) we can spin out many more possible future scenarios than we can think through critically, and 2) since L2 has no direct links to external reality, L2 has no built-in error detection that checks against reality. Even though L2 will sometimes casually apply some of its own rules to check things, this is an informal and incomplete process that generally relies on nothing more than feelings based largely on our mood, to tell us that such-and-so is more or less likely than some other thing because of whatever.

The prediction process is so notoriously unreliable that it has always featured prominently in literature, in the form of characters who have large dreams and a ridiculously unrealistic assessment of their abilities. This imbalance pushes them to heights of giddy expectation as they dream that their wild schemes will succeed perfectly, and then drives them to the depths of despair when their ill-considered plans crash to earth. This is typified in the gambler's attitude that cycles wildly between boundless, manic hope, and black despair in defeat.

Both of these following statements are true: 1) our mind cannot make rational, reliable predictions unless it uses a formal language, and 2) we cannot help but make predictions, all day, everyday, in our regular, informal language.

What our mind can do, which we take for prediction, is:

- say that the current situation will lead to a particular future based solely on our evaluation that it matches a pattern we think applies;
- know with certainty, based only on our emotional state, that the current `situation` *must* lead to a specific future `situation`;
- project, based on known patterns that match the current one (to whatever degree pleases us), that any number of future `situations` might happen;
- argue passionately, based on L0 moral truths, or L1 experience, that specified `situations` must inevitably lead to a certain dire or delightful future.

The key to why L2 predictions work at all, even with

this doubtful pedigree, is that we live in ecological and cognitive bubbles, inside of which the unusual is actually rare, and where familiar things and events generally end up in the usual way. This means that we can expect the current situation to be similar to previous situations, and that it will lead to familiar conclusions. Sometimes.

In adolescence, we are still often terribly surprised at how things turn out because our library of experiences is still much too small to cover the normal range of situations. Once we get into our late twenties or early thirties, we usually have enough experience, and we have situated ourselves deeply enough into a life, that the number of times we are completely surprised by experience falls to a relatively low level. This makes our 'predictions' of future events in our own life seem more reliable.

The other side of the problem with L2 predictions comes from the type of query that L2 is hardwired to execute to find potential futures from known patterns. It goes something like this:

```
find all patterns where the start situation
is more than x similar to the given situa-
tion, then sort results by similarity on
field q
```

Without even knowing that we are running a query, let

alone how to structure one, our mind lets us fill in both x and q any way we want. Since, in informal language, our mind uses comparatives, instead of quantitative parameters, when we say the similarity should be: any at all, some, moderate, or high, this could equate to 5%, 15%, 50%, or 75% similarity. In other words, it is up to us what we will accept in the range of mostly dissimilar to mostly similar results, which will obviously have a huge effect on the quantity and quality of results we get.

For the field parameter, there is nothing to say that we have to focus on the most important field, or even any of the important fields. We have all seen instances where people claim that *this* matches *that* based on the flimsiest pretext related to the most incidental detail (think conspiracy theories).

As a result, when we run queries against our L2 pattern memory, we usually get a crap ton of results that we think might predict the future. It's then entirely up to us to sift through the debris and choose which one we decide to go with, for whatever reason we want. This is how the informal prediction process works, how it is built to work, no matter how brilliant any of us thinks we are. And this is how scientists think, too, no matter how they dress it up, and unless they are using a proven formula to predict a future condition, they're just winging it as ineptly as we are.

The key idea to remember here is that L2 evolved as a predictor of physical reality events, but we try to use it to predict semantic reality events, something that is almost entirely beyond its capacity. This is why we can predict certain classes of physical events pretty well, but are so bad at predicting events in semantic reality.

The reason that such a poor prediction mechanism can survive natural selection, is because, after we have learned from our parents, and gotten some experience with life, it is likely that, when it matters most, we will be able to match the current situation with a known one pretty closely. This allows us to instantly disregard irrelevant results. When dealing with known risks, we can set the x and q parameters high enough to get back a solid plan that will enable us to start reacting before the crisis hits.

The other side of the prediction game is that the more remote, unfamiliar, or unimportant the situation is, the more frivolous our prediction of the future can be without actually killing us, or causing us great harm in the present. It goes without saying that the more abstract a situation is, the more removed from proven experience, the sillier our queries will be, and the more unreliable our predictions will be.

Our ability to anticipate the future is crucial to our survival, but our ability to predict abstract futures isn't worth spit. For example, everyone should know that the proper domain of science is measurement, but yet, in the quest for celebrity, almost all scientists will push beyond the realm of science to discuss *meaning*, and to declare the need for specific policies to mitigate possible future problems. But when they do this, they are crossing the line from science to demagoguery, even if they are wearing a lab coat at the time, because, believe it or not, lab coats don't actually know anything, and wearing them doesn't actually make you smarter.

Our ability to predict the *known* depends on many things, primarily formal methods, experience and diligence, but our ability to predict the *unknown* is essentially zero, because L2 doesn't have the capacity to do that (L3 does, but it takes a lot of work, a *lot*). Oh, and our ability to predict the future in non-linear dynamic systems is nil.

Making predictions on top of bad, or untested, models is also a recipe for failure. When our model is completely wrong for the reality of the situation, predictions are just projections from a present that doesn't exist to a future that will never be.

The L2 pattern object gives us a limited, but vital, ability to make pretty good *situational* predictions in familiar conditions. It does not equip us to make *strategic* predictions. Furthermore, it is only suitable for making predictions in regular problem spaces, and is entirely unsuited for making predictions in irregular problem spaces.

As shown in *Ultrareasoning*, all problems can be expressed quantitatively, and once in that form, predictions can be tested against quantified conditions. No generally valid predictions can be made from the internal, subjective ideas and feelings that fill our L2 patterns and thoughts. Reliable predictions can only be made using externalized ideas that are expressed as executable models. Everything else is just a guess.

Chapter 11

Problem Solving

Scientists and engineers are good at solving technical problems. They're good at developing ever more complex technology that is increasingly powerful and useful. Unfortunately, their impressive problem solving ability comes to a crashing halt at the border between the world of physical things and the world of thoughts, feelings, needs, and message communication.

There are five really good, and really big reasons why their problem solving abilities are so outstanding in one area, and yet so hopeless in the other:

1. regular problem solving techniques only work in regular problem spaces,

2. the mortality problem space is an irregular problem space,

3. things and ideas are very different,

4. some solutions can be exact, while others can only be optimizations, and

5. the world of ideas is much more complex than the world of things.

If we look at these issues one at a time, by the end, you should clearly understand why our problem solving ability falls short at the exact moment we get to the issues that we care about the most.

Problem Spaces & Problem Types

Problems exist in problem spaces. A problem space is the product of the physical and intellectual resources available for use in developing a solution to a problem. Think of a problem space as the combination of your knowledge and everything you have in your workshop that you can use. For example, as a teenager working as a mechanic in a service garage, the problem space I had for fixing cars included:

- my boss's and coworker's knowledge,
- the auto manuals for the cars I worked on,
- car lifts,
- my knowledge,

- the full tool chest,

- specialized tools in the shop,

- an oxy-acetylene torch.

Notice that there was no welding equipment. I could use the torch and brass rods to braze something like an exhaust pipe, or I could use the torch to heat a frozen nut or fitting, but I could not fix any problem that required welding. So, welding was not part of my problem space, meaning it could not be part of a problem solution. The shop also did not have any machining equipment, and I wouldn't know how to use it anyway, but I could take heads, brake drums, and blocks to a machine shop to do the work, so machining was included in my problem space, even though I had to pay someone else to do the work.

The point of a problem space is that if it lacks the resources to solve a problem, then you can't solve the problem. Sometimes, you can go out and get the knowledge, equipment, or resources to expand the problem space to allow you to fix the problem, but oftentimes, we lack the awareness, motivation or determination to do that, and our range of solutions is artificially and unnecessarily constrained by our meager problem space.

In *General Problem Theory*, I explain the difference between regular problem spaces and irregular problem spaces in detail. The short version is that exact solutions are available in regular problem spaces, but only optimization solutions are possible in irregular problem spaces. Think of a regular problem space as a rectangular space that can be perfectly tiled with square solution tiles, while an irregular problem space is an area enclosed with a fractal border as irregular as a shoreline that can never be perfectly tiled.

Historically, science is the discipline of externalizing internal solutions to problems in regular problem spaces, which are only a small subset of irregular problem spaces. The reason science hasn't succeeded in solving any of the big human, social problems is because scientists have been working strictly in regular problem spaces. The scientific method has to be enhanced to work in irregular problem spaces before it can begin to address problems in semantic reality. This is important because life problems constitute a superset of mortality related resource acquisition and management problems. The mortality problem space is an irregular problem space in which all problems are optimization problems that have no perfect solution. Such problems are described by the optimization formula:

Optimization Formula: alter some of the processes involved in a situation to optimize resource allocation for the benefit of chosen stakeholders. In mixed notation,[1] the formula looks like this:

$$alter(p_i...p_n) \rightarrow optimize(q_{i..n}) \rightarrow benefit(a_{i..n})$$

Pretending that problems in the mortality problem space can be solved with simple right or wrong solutions, like problems in a regular problem space, is wildly simplistic at best, consciously dishonest at worst, and flatly incompetent in any case.

The optimization formula even applies to solving problems at the level of the individual, because even when alone, we are complex systems with competing internal interests that can never all be fully satisfied at the same time.

One of the inherent difficulties that characterizes the mortality problem space is that solutions are time sensitive to such a degree that rerunning a process immediately after it produces a solution will not necessarily generate the same solution again, since the inputs can change moment by moment.

Before now, no one knew either that mortality problem spaces existed, or that all subjective problems can and must be expressed in the optimization formula in order

---

[1] See *Ultrareasoning*, chap. 30, for details.

to be solved in a verifiable way. The reason we haven't been able to solve any of the big problems before now is because we hadn't evolved enough to confidently use the L3 intellect as the problem solving engine that it is.

Realities

The world of things and the world of ideas are two actual, separate realities. Both are real, both are important, and, even though one is built on top of the other — like the law office on the seventeenth floor of an office building and the cafe on the ground floor — they are completely independent of each other, and quite incapable of doing each other's job.

Once you get a handle on the formal definition of reality, the concept of separate realities is easy to understand. Up until now, science and technology have been mostly restricted to the world of things, of physical reality. Ideas, feelings, needs, and human relations belong to the world of abstract ideas and message-based social connections, i.e., to semantic reality.

These are two different realities that are made up of different elements that interact in completely different ways. Solving a problem in one reality doesn't touch the problems in the other reality, and it doesn't equip you to solve problems in the other reality. This means that the way we calculate truth in one reality cannot be the same as the way we calculate truth in the other, since they are not even related.

Truth is important because we use it to determine whether or not a statement about something can be relied on if we decide to act on it. If a statement is true, then we can expect that actions based on it could work as expected, while if it's false, the action is much more likely to fail since it's not starting from where it needs to.

This is all well and good, but how do we verify that something is true? Simple, we apply a truth test that we are comfortable with, such as: belief, experience, evidence, authority, or formal, independent verification. Except for the last, these tests are pretty weak gruel to stake your life on, but that's what we've been doing since the beginning, with varying results.

The problem of verifying truth starts, of course, with the fact that **we think inside our head**, so what we have to do is figure out which of our internal ideas actually match something outside of us in reality, and to what degree. The best way to do this is to express our idea in formal terms, and get independent verification of its accuracy, but this is impractical in real life. In practice, we usually rely on belief, authority, experience, or scientific metaphor.

The problem with this is that, however careless our truth test is, we use the same process for both physical and semantic reality. What happens when you apply the concept of truth from one reality to another? The result is undefined, which means that anything can happen. Sound familiar? It should, because that's exactly what happens everyday when we apply reasoning we learned from the physical world to the world of ideas: anything can happen, and it often does, very much to our surprise.

How do we test truth in semantic reality in practice? Unfortunately, we rely on affirmation or rejection from the members of our cohort in the relevant group. We use belief, experience, documentation, authority, or faux scientific reasoning to form our idea, but we test it in practice with consensus or group approval. In other words, we move with the crowd, like a fish in a school of fish. Not exactly the the best test of truth.

Instead of using tests that actually apply to the world of ideas and meaning, we test truth in semantic reality the same way we do in physical reality. But there is a significant difference in that physical reality bruises us when we are wrong in ways semantic reality does not. So, no matter how obtuse we may be, there is pressure from physical reality to be at least partially right. But, since semantic reality is abstract, and only exists in the world of ideas and social agreements, there is nothing beyond social pressure to correct us. When we make a false claim in semantic reality, we can often completely evade responsibility for it by blaming the error on others. Remember, truth in semantic reality is measured by the change in the strength of social bonds, and anything that strengthens the bonds is true in the short term. When we lie in physical reality, correction can be brutal, but lying in semantic reality, if done well, can be quite rewarding.

Because we do not test truth correctly in semantic reality, we are frequently surprised and disappointed by the way things turn out. This comes up a lot in cases where we thought that someone was telling us the truth, when actually they were just lying for their own benefit. This happens so often it might be the norm, yet somehow we are nevertheless surprised by it, because we tested the truth of their words in a way that didn't even take into account the possibility that self-interest was warping their words and deeds.

Competent problem solving in semantic reality must,

at the very least, start out with a serious truth test that applies to the elements and forces in that reality, instead of trying to use an unrelated truth test. This means that we need tests that accurately measure both group strength and resource distribution among stakeholders, and that we use those tests to set a baseline before implementing a solution, and continue to use them to measure our progress so that we can adjust our solution as we go.

Our historical failure to solve any of the larger philosophical, ethical, moral, or political problems can clearly be traced, in large part, to our use of the wrong truth test in semantic reality reasoning. It makes you wonder what our humanities academics have been doing for the last thousand years that was so important that it kept them from ever discovering the fairly simple truth that semantic reality is different than physical reality.

Complexity

Why, after all these years, and all the attempts made by all the philosophers who eagerly added their two cents, haven't we been able to make any real progress in answering some, or even just one, of the pinnacle questions?[2] The answer to that should be clear by now: we have never had

---

[2]*Pinnacle Questions.*

any of the tools necessary even to understand the nature of the problems, let alone begin to answer them. But, that changes now, because now, at least, we know about problem spaces and separate realities, so at least we can begin to frame the questions.

Of course, as is usually the case, there is yet another barrier in front of us that we have to get around before we can begin working on solutions. This last barrier is that the problems we are talking about solving are inherently much, much more complex than the simple problems that theoretical physics can handle. It's not just that the problems are harder, it's that their essential complexity is orders of magnitude greater than any problem that can exist in physical reality.

Think about it for a minute. Physical reality is a simple system with about a hundred elements and a handful or two of forces that interact at or above the subatomic level in regular, predictable ways.[3] Semantic reality, on the other hand, is a synthetic, abstract reality that has no upper bound of complexity limiting the interactional structures that can be developed. While atomic elements in physical reality are what they are, and the forces acting on them are what they are, every single element in

---

[3]Worry about weird interpretations of quantum mechanics on your own time.

the optimization formula is related to independent actors who can, and do, change the nature and intensity of their needs and efforts continuously, which means that the inputs to all related equations can change while the equation is being worked.[4] The formulas describing semantic reality are fluid at all times. It's not just that the future is unpredictable, it's that the present, itself, is fluid.

In physical reality, a ball bounces as it does until wear and tear slowly degrades the conditions and the resulting bounce. Nothing like this exists in semantic reality. On the contrary, in this system of volition and meaning, the ball could *decide*, on its own, to bounce differently each time it touched the surface.

So, what reasoning tools can we use to tackle such complex problems? By now, we know that the different levels of our mind use their own structures and functions to solve problems in their own way. This allows us to list the main tools/approaches used by each level:

L0: makes decisions using interest-based `beliefs`;

L1: makes decisions using interest-based evaluation of `experience`;

L2: makes decisions based L0, L1 interest. L2 argues

---

[4]Yes, we parameterize these inputs for simulations, and can produce fixed results for the full range of inputs, but this is still not the same as predicting a particular event.

for that interest using rhetoric based on logic and consistency;[5]

L3: can solve optimization problems with explicit, parameterized inputs:

- costs & benefits

- stakeholders: winners and losers

- conditions & tests

- timeline to test and reevaluation

- viable and productive truth test.

L0 arguments, though primitive, are remarkably on point much of the time since they represent time-tested organizational solutions to mortality issues. Yes, they are old and static, but until the environment changes beyond recognition, these traditional solutions will almost always be better than what the educated elite will ever suggest. As for helping to tackle the big problems, L0 is incapable of contributing anything new.

L1 arguments are based on experience, and their usefulness will be limited only by how much the present is fundamentally different than the past. Since many of the fundamentals will only change slowly, L1 arguments will likely be useful in maintaining the status quo, but will not be helpful for cultivating or utilizing innovation.

---

[5]L2 can reason in formal languages, but the only way to arrive at a decision is the process mentioned above.

L2 reasoning is what we have relied on for all of our problem solving throughout the entire span of civilization. While L2 pattern-based reasoning helps us to understand physical reality, until we generate a library of patterns to describe the nature and function of semantic reality, it can't help us to explore and discover the unknown anymore than it has before, which is to say, not at all.

It's important to grasp that rhetoric, the most noble gas produced by the flatulent university, doesn't have any place in high level problem solving. On the contrary, where rhetoric appears, high level reasoning withers.

We need the L3 long-form query[6] and model-oriented reasoning to explore the unknown. These methodologies can open the way for us to discover new principles and techniques that will be able to support problem solving in irregular problem spaces. All problems that involve competing interests can be mapped to an optimization formula that is required to solve problems in irregular problem spaces. Problems with no competing stakeholders can be solved with simple solutions that are right or wrong, because such problems fit into regular problem spaces in which perfect solutions are possible. But, by the very nature of mortality and competing interests, there is no per-

---

[6]*General Problem Theory.*

fect solution to a problem in a mortality problem space.

Fixed resource allocation, based on a fixed value system, creates fixed rationing systems in regular problem spaces that have no competing stakeholders, so it can work in dictatorships as long as the tyrannical state controls everything. But, this reduces the problem to an exercise in coming up with a plan that rations resources from a fixed inventory to a fixed set of recipients who are not allowed to complain. This is not a very hard thing to do.

But, mortality interests change moment by moment, so any problem involving mortality interests has constantly changing inputs, so solutions can never be perfect or unchanging, since not all interests align, and all interests change over time. Mortality interests cannot converge over time because living beings occupy space, and the distribution of resources takes effort and time, so it is physically impossible for all needs to be satisfied simultaneously, even if a mythical perfect solution could ever be found.

Resource allocation becomes a difficult, irregular problem the instant you take into account the fact that the pool of resources is never adequate to satisfy everyone, and not all of it is available for distribution since it is reduced when some of it is used to maintain state power, some used to create the next pool of resources to be allocated, and some of it saved against bad times.

Furthermore, if the actual or perceived needs of your stakeholders change (a certainty), or if they can define their needs themselves, then this becomes a problem with a high order of irregularity that demands a constantly adjusting optimization solution, which, difficult as it is to create, won't even begin to guarantee that your customers will be satisfied at all times.

The evolution of L2 enabled us to create communication-based communities that, along with the scientific method, go a long way to making our problems in physical reality manageable. But, this solution to the challenges of physical reality inadvertently created a new level of complexity in semantic reality, a universe far more complex than the original one whose problems it was created to solve.

What's the solution? Study model-oriented reasoning,[7] and learn how to use these tools well enough to build beautiful theories, techniques, and solutions. Once they exist, L3 problem solving skills can be patternized and made available to everyone, but first they have to be invented, tested, and proven.

Until then, we're kind of screwed.

---

[7] *Ultrareasoning, The Structure of Truth, General Problem Theory,* and *Super Stupid.*

Chapter 12

Free Will

It's hard to take the question, "Do we really have free will?" seriously. I mean, the whole "it's all fate" thing is just patently ridiculous. I guess the attraction to it is the dream that our little self could be so important, among the billions of souls who have ever lived, that someone *up there* would take the time to plan out our life. That would make us seem important, wouldn't it?

The other factor driving the debate, though, is the total, utter, and complete ignorance that people have of how our mind really works. I guess if you miss the fact that we are evaluation-decision engines, you might wonder what possessed us to make *that* decision on *that* particular day. But, if you understand anything about how our mind works, surely you know that our mind is little more than a mechanism that does nothing but execute scan-seek-perceive-evaluate-act cycles all day long, every day of our life.

As a lower bound, I would estimate that we repeat this cycle at least 9,000 times a day, everyday. That makes 229,950,000 decisions we make in 70 years. Given that, it hardly seems fair to question only one of them without questioning all of them. I mean, if fate intervened in one decision we remember as a turning point, why not all, or at least in 1% (that's 2,229,500) of our decisions?

It is said that there are approximately 10^{80} atoms in the entire universe. That's a lot of atoms, and I mean, *a lot*. If you write it out, it look like this:

$100,000,000,000,000,000,000,000,000,000,000,$
$000,000,000,000,000,000,000,000,000,000,000,$
000

That's a whole lot of zeroes, but the way I do the math, the number of different external and internal sensory permutations that we are equipped to evaluate into an action command, something we do hundreds or thousands of times a day is:

$$10, 000, 000, 000, 000, 000, 000, 000, 000, 000, 000, 000, 000,$$

$$000, 000, 000, 000, 000, 000, 000, 000, 000, 000, 000, 000, 000,$$

$$000, 000, 000, 000, 000, 000, 000, 000$$

And that's even more zeroes. This means that there are potentially a whole lot more different kinds of input that can go into our normal decisions than there are atoms in the universe.

Now, maybe my assumptions or calculations are wrong, not an uncommon event, I admit, but I think I am being pretty conservative in estimating that, if we scale the evacule model up to life size, that there might be as many as:

2000 sight evacules

500 sound evacules

2000 smell evacules

500 touch evacules

500 taste evacules

20 internal senses, each with 200 evacules

The way I do the math, if we say there are 10 possible values in each of the 3 positions in the evacule, we actually come up with about 10^{106} different permutations.

But, even if there are only a tenth of that many, say

10^{12} different permutations, that's still a trillion possible different sensory inputs that we evaluate all day, every day, and convert down into an approach-retreat-ignore action command.

Given that, it just seems odd that anyone would ever ask the question, "Why did I make that decision, to take that action, at that moment, on that day?" Why did we decide to go right, instead of left? We did it because that was the outcome of our ordinary calculation of how to respond to a particular set of sensory inputs, that's all. Whether it went well or ill for us is simply part of the risk of being a volitionally mobile creature.

Does this mean that there couldn't be some extrasensory input at a particular moment on a particular day that flipped the critical bit that cascaded through enough changes to switch us from moving to the right, to moving to the left, instead? No, that's entirely possible, and if believing it happened that way helps us to deal with reality, then that's fine. But to take it seriously as a philosophical question, when we never before even had a model to explain how we make the most mundane decision to take the most ordinary action from an unremarkable perception, well, it just seems to be silly, and a wasteful distraction from the brief opportunity our life gives us to actually learn something and contribute to our civilization.

Are we constrained by our social situation? By our ties to friends, family, religion, and work? It depends on the individual case, of course, and our spectrum of choices certainly can be limited by such ties as we accept, or cannot escape, but this hardly amounts to fate. The less we take control of our own life, the less we do control our own life, and the less we can control our own fate, but that's obvious.

The point to the little numerical exercise above was to emphasize the sheer number of choices we make in a normal day that, in the end, contribute to defining the life we ultimately live. Boiling our whole life down to a simple concept or value judgment, whether it be to fate, or just saying that we're all good or all bad, is an example of the intellectual sin of oversimplification. If it would take you days or weeks, or longer, to explain all of the details and complexity of your life to someone else, and to do it well enough so that they could finish your next sentence for you, then how much of your truth would be lost if you boiled your entire life down to a phrase or a word, such as fate?

The real flaw in the argument about fate is the claim that opportunity w inevitably leads to distant future xyz, which it most assuredly does not. Perhaps you were hoping to be unexpectedly thrust into the spotlight and given an opportunity to pursue a life on stage? Does that lead to you getting all of your life dreams fulfilled? No, because life is more complicated than that, and dreams change. Maybe one aspect of your life fulfills your dreams, but the rest of your dreams have to be nurtured, and require actions from other people to come true, actions that they may not be willing or able to do at the right time.

The point to this is not to say whether or not you should believe that a higher power helps to guide your life, that's up to you, and there's nothing wrong with believing that. The point is that we are decision making machines, that's what we do, that's what we are built for. We interpret sensory input and decide how to move so as to maximize our chances for survival. Sometimes we survive, and one time we will die. This is certain. This is the essence of our existence, we evaluate, we decide, we act.

We do not need any supernatural intervention to do what we do every minute of every day we are alive and awake. But, if you want to believe that some higher power is helping you to make the right decision in a given situation, that is up to you. Any belief that is viable and productive is valid, at least for now. Any belief that costs you more in elevated risk or lost opportunity than it returns to you in options and resources, is a bad deal, but one that you can choose to make, if you want.

We have free will to interpret, decide, and act. If, through our own shortcomings, we have a severely restricted vocabulary of terms in which to think, then our decisions and actions will be constrained within a very small compass of the vast field of possibilities available to us. But, that's on us, the nature of cognition is that we assemble and extend the vocabulary of ideas we can use to think, and if we choose not to do that, then we are living in a prison of our own making.

We are an organism that processes internal and external sensory input into movement solutions to mortality problems. The persistence of our species is proof that this works pretty well. To suppose that fate guides our path, rather than mortality related decisions, ignores the fact that we only survive as long as those decisions are made correctly, in our interest, in a timely fashion.

The **error exceeds content** law virtually assures that the worlds we live in will often be confusing and mysterious. Add to that our inability to discriminate between different realities, and it becomes certain that events in reality will sometimes seem like they are being guided by mysterious, invisible forces from another dimension. In the past, we haven't known enough about how our mind works to understand that the dimension that these mysterious forces come from is actually inside of largely invisible regions of our own mind.

Chapter 13

Attitude

In case you haven't noticed it yet, we're developing kind of a theme here: instead of looking at a trait or behavior through a psychological or developmental lens, we look beneath its surface and focus on the structures and functions underlying it. This approach can be used to examine any of our behaviors, and perhaps an encyclopedia of behaviors will be compiled sometime in the future, but for now, we'll start by looking at a very familiar, often annoying behavior: attitude. `Attitude` is an affectation that is simultaneously trivial, immature, and ever-present, but which we usually dismiss with just an irritated shrug when we experience it in others.

Of course, there are all different kinds of attitudes, from bad to good, with all possible degrees of power and significance, but for our current purposes we will confine our attention to the particular `attitude` that tries to get the most attention, the one that adolescents and hip, young adults proudly wear like gang colors: the alienated `attitude`, a surly, petulant pose characterized by a high n and a fixed a, p. For this discussion, we'll match the high non-self value with a medium to high anti-self dimension, and a medium to low positive dimension. The precise values of each are not important, just their relation to each other.

We are looking deeper into the `attitude` phenomenon to demonstrate how much more we can learn about human feelings and behavior, both ours and others, if we take the time to carefully apply the model we have been discussing to *any* facet of the human experience we are interested in. `Attitude` is just an example.

What An Attitude Is

Without going into all of the detail explained elsewhere[1], we'll start the discussion of `attitude` with an examination of the structures involved.

The first thing you have to figure out when you are

---

[1] *Ultrareasoning: Principles and Practices of Faceted Model-Oriented Reasoning.*

trying to understand how a particular facet of the mind works is, how does it handle facts? You'd think that this would force you to define what a **fact** is first, but it turns out not to be so. Merely trying to answer the question actually causes a definition of sorts to emerge in the process. In this particular case, the concept of exigent facts and deferrable facts emerged from the exploration.

Exigent facts are those that demand your attention right now, and these are handled by L0 and L1. Deferrable facts are those that don't have to be handled immediately, and most of the input we get from communication with others fits into the deferrable category. According both to the model and our own experience, L2 handles deferrable facts as time allows, sometimes even days later. It makes sense that deferrable facts get put at the bottom of the to-do list to be handled by the slowest of the first three intellect levels.

From this categorization, it's clear that facts are merely statements with some kind of truth value that ranges from undefined to false to true. Traditionally, we have used facts as a crutch to maintain the illusion that L0 truth applies to everything, because this implies that we can understand everything. But by now, we should all know better than to believe that.

Unlike exigent facts, deferrable facts can be meaningless, or may only become important much later. This means that some or all deferrable facts can be ignored, at least for now. This is important, because there is simply not enough time and resources available to contemplate every deferrable fact. What, then, can we do? How do we manage the torrent of facts we get from all sources in our incoming message streams, all day, everyday?

One of the possible ways to handle information overload is simplicity itself: we just ignore deferrable facts. In actuality, this is our primary strategy for managing information overload, and the main two mechanisms that we use to ignore deferrable content are the `attitude` and the `opinion`. As explained before, the `opinion` object sorts input in a way that allows us to stay on course, and it works very well, but sorting takes work, and work takes time and effort, time that we often do not have, and effort that we are not always willing to expend.

Enter the `attitude` object, which discards deferrable facts with a null operation that takes no time, requires no engagement, and raises no questions. In programming, this is called a bit bucket, where you can send streams of output to disappear. This leaves what seems to be an empty and useless pattern, but what it actu-

Attitude Object
description
evaluation link
action(null)
rules (null)
patterns (null)

Table 13.1: Attitude Object

ally creates is an extremely powerful and important container pattern that both utilizes and depends on this bare, skeletal structure. The way the `attitude` object does this is pretty slick: it's a pure container pattern with a lightweight structure, shown in table 13.1, which makes it highly performant, since it doesn't do much, and what little it does do, will execute virtually instantaneously. In the `attitude` container pattern, most of the fields are null, there is no action to be done, and the evaluation field is just a link to an archetypal high n evacule in L0.

The only important elements in the attitude pattern object are the description and evaluation link. The resulting structure supports a named evaluation of a set of patterns that has no size limit, since they are instantly discarded, not saved. The way that the attitude object works is that an active attitude can process any deferrable fact instantaneously to allow the mind to maintain its level of focus on the dynamic sensorium, i.e., the world around it, without having to lose any time in reflection or consideration. Powerful attitudes can digest any deferrable fact, but lesser, more limited attitudes only process facts related to a given topic.

The n dimension determines how much an attitude ignores. What makes `attitude` process facts so fast is that it implements the view that thoughtfulness and consideration are both unnecessary and futile in processing deferrable facts, because the end result, the end evaluation of the current situation, is already known once an attitude is invoked, because it is the evaluation in the attitude. Think about it for a minute: we all use attitude, to a greater or lesser degree, all the time, and somehow it suffices to enable us to process input successfully enough for us to survive. You must admit, a shortcut that essentially saves virtually all the work needed to process experience, is kind of brilliant.

How could this work? It works because understanding is achieved when the relation of *other* to *self* is defined by linking a fact to a value assignment in L0. `Attitude` lets us evaluate input without examining it. Given that, the quickest way, then, to understand something is to invoke an attitude that matches our mood to instantaneously make sense of any experience. The motto of `attitude`

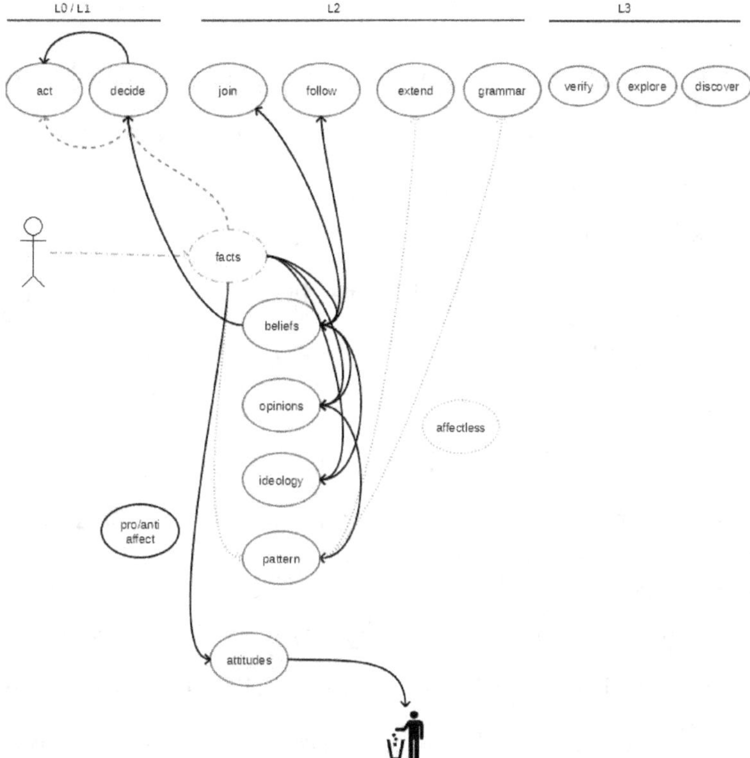

Figure 13.1: Communication paths, objects and functions.

could be: *frequently wrong, but always fast.*

In figure 13.1, the line that connects facts (initially perceived by the figure on the left) directly to the trash through an attitude, instead of extracting meaning from it, illustrates how **attitude** differs from other L2 structures.

Attitudes are most glaringly apparent when they are flaunted like peacock plumage by adolescents and young adults who aspire to seem older, more in the know, or more powerful than they actually are. But, to be sure, attitudes are used by, and evident in, all age groups. If you doubt this, watch the nightly news from any source: its function is to make sense of the day's events by applying an attitude that will comfortably contextualize all events, from the normal to the bizarre, from the wholesome to the macabre, into the editorial narrative being pushed by management.

The effect of attitude is perhaps best illustrated by the Wisdom Fallacy, the presumption that we can use arcane knowledge of some hidden or supernatural force to insulate ourself from the trials and tribulations of the mundane, earthly plane. The wisdom attitude dismisses the troubles of diurnal life with the assessment that such trivialities can be disregarded as unimportant, simply because they pale in comparison to the significance of the arcana of the wisdom culture. This attitude is assiduously cultivated by religious, intellectual, political, and cultured power groups.

The wisdom attitude even arises spontaneously in the youth culture of every new generation, disguised as the 'cool', detached, invulnerable attitude, which is used as a tool to quell the anxiety triggered by the prospect of having to make one's own way in the wide world outside of the family. Adults use the facade of detached indifference to fence off those areas of reality that they could never master.

The function of an attitude is to maintain a particular state of mind, regardless of events in any reality. Strong `attitudes` act as an energy efficient way to move through life with a minimum of interaction or engagement, since they save you the trouble of even considering, let alone examining, any new input, whether it be person, message, or belief.

Conveniently, the evidence supporting your attitude is your own evaluation of your own experience. Thus, it is a tautology. To test this, ask anyone who is displaying any attitude, at any time, why that attitude is correct in this situation, and all you will get back is an incoherent hodge-podge of anecdotes and affect, the refutation of which will never suffice to invalidate the attitude itself. Remember, attitude is a data management, not a semantic, function. Attitude has nothing to do with content, but everything to do with rapid data processing and maintenance of the current mental state.

Imagine you are facing a high-speed, unlimited capacity, tennis ball serving machine: which would be easier, to try to return every ball in bounds, or just to bat them away to avoid being hit? Remember, attitude processes only deferrable facts; immediately impactful facts are ordinarily handled through other channels.

There are positive attitudes, negative attitudes, resigned, and dismissive attitudes, just to name a few. Attitudes are formed at the nexus of constitution and experience, where our sense of power, or powerlessness, to control the outcome of events, is formed. However, they are not a psychological development, and to think that they are actually reflects the attitude that, but for psychological injury, behavior is always normative. But, this is not a rational idea — even though an entire discipline is built on it — it is actually just an *attitude* of conceit and control that asserts that our word-idea mind can defeat the chaos of experience.

In general, what we would call negative attitudes are adopted to cope with a repeated failure to successfully change the course of events to one's liking, while positive attitudes are bred from experiencing a history of empowerment and success. Negative attitudes tamp down your expectations and justify disengagement, while positive attitudes are more likely to stimulate engagement and hope. Even though, under normal circumstances, positive attitudes tend to be more productive than negative ones, neither is better than the other, since they are both just dismissive disposal algorithms, and the price of having them will be different in different situations. After all, sometimes you have to fight, and sometimes it's best just to run away.

Attitudes are essentially skeletal, secular beliefs, beliefs without a specified source or a web of creed patterns, a belief stripped of all of its content except for the characteristic evaluation. Attitudes are faster operations than belief, so fast, in fact, that where a belief is generally only applied to facts after they have been examined, attitudes can determine how the fact is evaluated in the first place.

An attitude is distinguished from a mood by its function: attitudes dispose of facts, while mood colors experience. One can have both a grumpy attitude and a grumpy mood, but the effect is different. A grumpy mood biases evaluation of experience, it filters experience through a particular evaluation, but the altered experience is then processed normally, whereas a grumpy attitude essentially dismisses input in order to preserve the current state of being by isolating the self from experience.

In general, if you assume a strong enough attitude, it empowers you to act as if you know all there is to know, as if you are above the fray, invulnerable, and surprise-proof.

Adopting the correct attitude can even give you an entrée into groups pushing that point of view.

Attitude and n are interdependent. High n evaluations make us cynical and defeatist and sour our attitude; a bad attitude drives us to evaluate perceptions with a high n alienation factor.

Since the function of an attitude is to discharge the potential of ideas to disturb our internal status quo, it precludes the consideration of input. For this reason, arguments with an attitude-possessed person cannot be regarded as rational discussions on any level. Attitudes act as defensive screens, so any intelligent discussion can only happen after attitudes have been dropped.

An attitude that is durable enough to be part of a personal lifestyle is both a measure and a determinant of one's willingness to engage in a given type of interaction.

I am not saying that you shouldn't use attitudes, nor even that you should avoid a particular one, although I have been harsh on the alienated attitude, and have tried to point out how much it costs in lost opportunities. "But," you might object, "the circumstances of my life have been so miserable that the only rational response is to take an alienated attitude towards all of life." My reply to this, without looking into the merits of your case, would be to point out again that your experience justifies your attitude because it's a tautology. Everyone's experience justifies their attitudes. But you aren't forced to accept that, and you aren't forced to stop trying to move forward.

Chapter 14

Reasoning Errors

In a way, this is the last chapter of the book. The following chapter, **The Origin of Language**, was actually written as the first chapter, but got moved to the end when I realized I had written it mostly for myself. It's the longest and most difficult chapter in the book, so I consider it to be extra credit. It's really interesting, and I think the thoughtful reader will gain a lot by working through it, but I'm not holding you to it. The actual last chapter, **Next**, is just kind of like a hand-out you get at the end of a conference that tells you about various resources you can use to extend your education. It's important, interesting, and short, so you should read it, but it doesn't introduce any new material.

That leaves this chapter, which might have been a

summary, but I decided to make it a list of practical lessons on reasoning, instead. Although not all the connections may be immediately obvious, these lessons do actually follow from the previous explanations of how the mind really works. It seemed to me that an easy list of dos and don'ts might be a more fun way to wrap things up instead of having to slog through a pedantic summary at the end.

So, the following is a short list of reasoning errors we all see in daily life that you should able to recognize if you've grokked how the mind really works.

Remember, these warnings only apply if you are actually trying to accomplish something in physical reality, either through group or individual effort. Of course, if all you are interested in doing is accumulating power in your group of choice, then there are no rules of reasoning you need to care about beyond the core truth of semantic reality: `at all costs, gain power and avoid losing it.`

1D - One Dimensional Analysis

Multidimensional systems cannot be adequately understood by simply looking at a single dimension. They must be analyzed along as many dimensions as are required to accurately describe and predict the system's behavior. In order to predictably produce outcomes with measurable improvements, solutions to problems in complex systems must also be multidimensional and specific.

All systems whose outputs cannot be shown to have a linear relation to their inputs are non-linear. The need to preserve dimensions in solutions to problems in non-linear dynamic systems is even greater than in linear dynamic systems precisely because their output is inherently unpredictable. The idea that we can predict the future state of non-linear dynamic systems (such as social, economic, or climate, to name a few) simply by plucking one factor from the sea of factors involved in the system, is ridiculous.

There is circuitry in our layered mind that is built around a path that reduces complex thought down to a simple evaluation that can be implemented as an action. The mental urge to reduce the complexity of dynamic systems down to a single factor, follows that path. The psychological need to follow this path aligns with our fear of the unknown and our need to flee, as quickly as possible, from uncertainty back to safety.

If we understand the term `intellectual` to imply some fidelity to rigor, results, and formal process, then we can say that there is no intellectual justification for prematurely hastening down this path. Nevertheless, since intellectuals know nothing about reasoning or how the mind is structured or really works, they instinctively compete to see how fast they can get from the abstract to the certain, and then boast of their speed like ten year old kids.

Anyone who reduces a complex system to a single dimension is not seeking truth in the world of actions and consequences in any reality, but is solely focused on competing for power in some semantic reality realm.

Limitations of Mathematics

Pure mathematics is a formal language with an undefined relation to external reality. Mathematicians all know this, but somehow it gets lost in translation to lay people in phrases like "mathematics is the language of nature". It's not. Applied mathematics is the subset of mathematics that has been shown to reliably describe observable phenomena in nature.

Why is this important? Unfortunately, some of the peculiarities of the formal language have colored our imagination and incorrectly framed our thinking in ways that sometimes drives us towards unfortunate conclusions. The best example of this is that there is no such thing as infinity in external reality, either physical or semantic. Infinity only exists in formal languages, and can only exist in formal reality. It is impossible for it to ever exist in the world of matter or social relations.

Another mismatch between pure mathematics and external reality is that in reality, there is no such thing as division by zero. It doesn't exist, it can't happen. That it exists in pure mathematics and is carried over to applied mathematics is a flaw, a limitation of the formal language.

A third mismatch between math and external reality is the class of ideas typified by the definition that two points define a straight line. This may be true in the abstract reality of formal languages, but since straight lines that extend infinitely in both directions cannot exist in external reality, it cannot be true in our world. In external reality, two points, under certain conditions, can define a straight line segment, or on a sphere they can define a geodesic, but they cannot define a straight line that is infinite. This may seem both obvious and trivial, but you'll soon see why it is important.

Sound, powerful formal languages are very good at externalizing ideas so that they can be tested against reality, whether the language is a programming language, or a branch of mathematics. Different formal languages model different problem domains better than others, but they are just tools, they aren't, in themselves, authoritative.

Were we to define a mathematics of physical reality, I would argue that it is likely that there would have to be a minimum unit of length to represent the reality that things smaller than a certain size do not seem to exist in our universe. Why pollute the purity of the language with constants? To make it a better language in its area of application. It seems that if we actually defined a dialect of mathematics to describe physical reality, we would exclude things that do not, and cannot, exist in the target domain.

Whether I am right or wrong in my predilections on this subject is a matter of no consequence. I bring up the subject simply to jolt us away from considering mathematics to be "true" in a way that it's not, because doing so pollutes and degrades our ability to think clearly.

Trend Thinking

Two points can define a line segment that extends between them, but what lies beyond those points in either direction is undefined. Sound abstract? It's not. Think about graphs and charts, the kind that ideologues, intellectuals, and pundits use to convince you that they know what the future will look like. They take a small number of data points, draw a line through them, and then they extend it out in the future to act as a trend line. Their argument is simple: if current conditions continue unchanged, then the future will certainly be a simple extension of the present. Except, current conditions *never* continue unchanged in either physical or semantic reality for very long.

Trend thinking is pure L2 pattern extension bunk. It is not scientific, it is not intellectually sound, and it is nearly always wrong, unless the time frame is so short that the future significantly overlaps the present. The only reason it is ever right is because anything that is not completely impossible is bound to happen at least once, for at least a moment.

Trend thinking is the main tool that L2 uses to make crappy predictions about the future. We're attracted to these kind of predictions because they are easy to make and understand, and they help us to feel more situated and confident, even if the prediction is dire. At least we *know* that terrible things are coming, and won't be caught off guard, right? But, as previously discussed, L2 predictions are, by design, really low quality, and trend thinking leads the way in stupid prognostication.

Backwards Reasoning

Ideologues, intellectuals in the humanities and soft sciences, and isolated, uneducated primitive people. What do they all have in common? They all use backwards reasoning to connect certainty to data without ever exposing their beliefs to challenge or disproof. Backwards reasoning begins with certainty, and ends with justification.

Why do they get away with this? Simple, their truth is defined solely by its affect on maintaining their position in their group, and facts in reality are irrelevant until they are impossible to ignore. But, even when the contradiction is impossible to ignore, rather than allow it to refute their backwards reasoning, they simply shift the point of certainty without even a nod of acknowledgment, and push forward again. As long as you remember that truth in semantic reality has nothing to do with physical reality, you should be able to understand this apparently contradictory situation.

Reasoning from conclusion to facts is not reasoning. Unless you are open to changing your position, you are not actually reasoning. This means that if you value your social status and lifestyle above the demonstrable truth — as nearly every one must — then whatever you are doing with your brain in pursuit of your goals has nothing to do with the kind of *reasoning* that interrogates reality.

Backwards reasoning is not reasoning, it is not inquiry in search of truth, it is defense of interest.

Meaning

Meaning is transgenerational value. Value is the L0 evaluation of mortality relevance. We can fully evaluate our own experience without the need for society or language. But, to define meaning, we need a way to project the value from our present effort and experience out beyond the confines of our lifetime. Defining meaning in life requires both language and one or more social units.

This may seem an unromantic way to define a concept so important as meaning, but cogency is the essence of clear definition. And what this cogent definition should make clear, even to academics, is that meaning is something you *do*, not something that you *receive*, or something that exists independent of your effort.

"There is no meaning in reality!" Any university student who says that should be expelled and consigned to a life of manual labor in the hope that they might, with a lot of supervision, eventually be able to pull their own weight.

Meaning is not something to be found on the ground, it is a power that must be laboriously knitted together of pieces of personal values, group values, and ultimate values. Meaning gives us the power to stay on course through the dark storms of real life as we slog towards our ultimate goal.

Only adolescents and failed adults think meaning is owed to them. It is not. Like any other capability, it is a power that can be cultivated and developed with effort, care, and skill. For a college student or academic to base their philosophy on their discovery that meaning does not exist in physical reality is a disqualifying offense.

Urgency

It's important to understand things like loopbacks and meaning precisely because these mechanisms will exist and operate in your mind whether or not you define them, believe in them, or accept them. If you decide that meaning is null, and that traditional loopbacks, such as god, are stupid, all this means is that some idiotic attitude of yours is going to be silently promoted to take the place of sound, historically proven solutions. Replacing a proven solution with a half-assed notion you came up with last night while smoking, will eventually just expose you to more frequent and severe uncontrolled swings of emotion that will exacerbate your feelings of alienation and purposelessness as chaotic thinking overwhelms your reasoning.

Either you define meaning in your life, or it will be defined for you. One of the first symptoms of a failure to define meaning is that random events and obligations suddenly seem urgent, like when you start to obsess about the implications of natural events and cycles that you cannot control.

When meaning is rejected, urgency and crisis, or depression and inertness, will fill the vacuum in your thoughts and feelings.

Scale Mismatch

While almost no one is trained to think in models instead of in mudball ideas, the brain, itself, necessarily organizes input into executable, discrete models. 'Discrete' refers to the fact that the models are populated with a few — typically a dozen or fewer — bits of information, rather the billions of bits that it would take to render a single tree in high fidelity. Each of these few data points has to be individually chosen, set into place, and remembered, in order to create a useful model of the thing we want to be able to think about. In other words, creating ideas of things that exist in reality is not free, and often not even cheap.

The **error exceeds content** law is merely a recognition of the fact that it is impossible for us ever to remember as much data about a thing as there are measurements that could be made of it, let alone understand and remember the exact state of the boundless number of relations among its elements that could be cataloged. We could look deeply into anything we think we know and be amazed at the level of detail we had previously missed.

But this is not a surprise, it is is definitional. We shouldn't draw idiotic conclusions from comparing the volume of the universe to the size of our brain. Rather than being stupefied by the obvious, it might be best to save your wonder for where it belongs: deep in the amazement at what our trained and disciplined mind can comprehend and do. It's not that the universe or whatever is so grand, but rather that our tiny brain has the capacity to measure, analyze, and understand it.

Law	Don't Do This
The mind cannot directly see inside of itself.	Assume that our word-thinking mind is the center of our mind, that it can see and understand the whole mind.
We think inside of our head.	Assume that internal ideas objectively describe external reality, assert that internal ideas do not need to be externalized to be validated.
Cognition is evaluation-based.	Assume that the purpose and natural function of cognition is to accumulate and correlate a limitless amount of correct knowledge.
Evaluation is at least tripolar.	Neglect the alienation dimension in your understanding of emotion and truth. Think that everything is either right or wrong
Perception is reductive.	Assume that our senses deliver an accurate and complete picture of reality separate from our interests.
Error exceeds content.	Assume that ideas inside our head accurately and fully represent external reality.

Table 14.1: UCM Laws Violations

Law Violations

Table 14.1 is a handy-dandy table of universal cognition model laws, and some of the typical ways we violate them. If you value quality thought, you might consider avoiding these errors.

Chapter 15

The Origin of Language

This chapter has been placed in the penultimate position because it is the longest chapter, and it requires the heaviest lifting. Presumably, having made it this far, you might be motivated to go a little further and tackle this very interesting and useful topic. If not, you've already succeeded in getting the gist of the book, so congratulations. But, if you're willing, you might find this last, longest climb to be well worth the effort. Have fun.

The `evacule` is the atom of evaluation, and is the basis of all language, just as it is the basis of all cognition. It encodes the hate-love-indifference tripole that is the hub of the language wheel that radiates outward along the three axes, through successive layers of seminal constructs, to undergird the entire, layered language landscape.

Most of our ideas and opinions are not the product of well thought out reasoning that dispassionately processes reality into coherent thought, but are, instead, the natural product of inherited, evolved structures and related lower level, pre-verbal functions. Most of our thoughts and conversations actually boil down to very simple, primordial sentences that map directly to pre-verbal constructs encoded in the evolved organic structures upon which our cognition is built, rather than being the product of educated ratiocination.

What we know as *language,* both the verbal and written form, is made up of higher level socio-verbal constructs that build on strong pre-verbal foundations that constrain and focus what we call *thoughts* into narrow channels of concern that coincide so closely with our mortality interests that we don't even suspect that they are different things. The word-language, in which we think and speak, sits on top of this pre-verbal foundation like the visible 10% of an iceberg sits on top of the submerged portion.

Verbal language *expresses* but does not *create* the content of most of the messages we transmit to each other about our internal thoughts and experiences. Message content derives from our internal experience of perceptions, events, and reactions, both internal and external. Since our mind evolved in layers, all of these language content elements arise from various levels of our evolved mind, not from a single, rational locus, as we unconsciously assume per the purblind defect. This essay will show which types of common thoughts/messages arise on which level of the mind, and what they mean both in context and in combination.

The larger question we are addressing is, *why haven't we been able to use our reasoning ability to solve the larger, harder problems?* The answer that this analysis will make clear is: *because we do not yet know how to reason at a high enough level to begin to successfully tackle high level problems.* A linguistic analysis will show that this is because most of our reasoning comes from lower intellect levels that aren't capable of processing higher level problems.

This situation has hitherto escaped our notice because, without an understanding of the layered nature and function of the mind, we have never had even a hope of understanding natural language, or the thoughts that are

formed in it. We mistakenly think that our thoughts
spring whole from some mystical higher reasoning function when, in reality, they arise from lower level structural
mechanisms that are directly related to our mortality interests.

In times past, pupils learned to diagram sentences according to parts of speech. Structural linguistic analysis
goes beyond that and gives us new options so that we can
now examine various common types of sentences to identify from which inherited layers of the mind they spring.
This enables us to contextualize the meaning of each clause
and sentence in order to better understand what the capabilities and constraints of our different types of thought
are. We can use a deep understanding of the origin and
nature of language to pierce through the rhetorical fog
spewed by would-be thinkers, and maintain a sharp focus
on real problems in order to be able to do a better job of
making progress on our higher pursuits, while preserving
our own interests and meaningful values.

Types Of Language

All language is about the recipient: the listener, the reader,
the viewer, the message processor, even the ramblings of

the narcissist whose focus on self is meant to elicit admiration without even acknowledging the listener. Language is inherently social in intent, but it can be either structural or social in origin.

We will be discussing four main types of language in this model: pre-verbal, informal, semi-formal, and formal.

Pre-verbal messages can be transmitted through body language using gestures, expressions, sounds, smells and actions (as well as words). The context of this level of communication is social grouping (herding, mating, and coupling are forms of grouping) or social separation.

Informal language is what we use everyday to think and to express feelings. It is suitable for ambiguously expressing affect or beliefs, and for marshaling followers or compatriots in a group endeavor. Informal language is ill-suited for expressing facts, because the value aspects of the language introduce an ineradicable aspect of imprecision that we know as *subjectivity* even when externalities are referenced. Language that is personal and capable of expressing our values, feelings, hopes and dreams is internal language, it is the language in which we think, and is `informal` to the extent that it is personal, value-laden, and internally focused. Informal language is about personal experience, self-interest, grouping, and the feelings related to grouping motivation or efficacy.

Semi-formal language uses references to external e-vents and phenomena that can, to some extent, be verified to exist in a reality external to the self. It can be used, for example, by co-workers to coordinate their efforts on a common project, using a combination of experiential and technical terms. Semi-formal language supports cooperating on tasks in an external reality.

Formal language has an unambiguously defined grammar and lexicon that is independent of personal values and context. It can be used to precisely express ideas about external reality[1] in such a way that assertions of predictable or reproducible phenomena can be independently verified. Formal language is uniquely useful in efforts to precisely describe external reality. However, even academics, scientists, and others who use formal language daily, struggle to understand its broader implications. It is worth noting that:

  a: very few people know, use, or understand the power of formal language;

  b: professionals conversant with one or more formal languages generally transgress the limits of formality in order to claim personal authority beyond the

---

[1]Any reality in $\Re$, including $\mathbb{F}$, the reality of formal languages.

limits of the language in unrelated fields, or in the subjective domain;

c: due mostly to a lack understanding about the nature of language and knowledge, almost no one understands the relation between formal and informal language.

The essence of a formal language is that the **context** and **goal** components of the **statement** construct are unambiguously defined and explicit, not implicit, undefined, or ill-thought out, as is the rule with informal language. The rigor of formal language is what allows other competent scholars to replicate experimental results.

In programming terms, formal languages have a predicate function that returns **true** if and only if the x being considered is actually an element of the set $\mathbf{X}$ defined in the language grammar.

$$p(x) = \mathtt{true} \iff x \in \mathbf{X}$$

Elsewhere, we have referred to this as an *indicator function* that defines set membership. The three non-formal types of language lack the necessary rigor to precisely define the line between included and excluded elements, and this makes them inherently imprecise and subjective.

Informal language is imprecise because its focus is primarily on expressing internal realities that contain value and meaning dimensions that cannot be externalized, instead of focusing strictly on measurable aspects of external phenomena. From a formal reasoning perspective, informal language is fallacious in its core because it conflates internal and external reality, and it does this with a passion that obviates any possibility of achieving the precision necessary to describe external reality in verifiable terms. In fact, the truth function we use to validate informal language is not verification at all, but a form of *agreement* that curries the assent of others to pretend that we are, for the moment at least, mutually immersed in a common reality that includes all of our internal realities together. But that reality does not, and cannot, ever actually exist.

Perception - Action Cycle Elements

The perception-action cycle: `perceive` $\rightarrow$ `evaluate` $\rightarrow$ `move`, evolved prior to the development of the individual levels of evolved cognition — perhaps even at the single cell level — and this cycle is the foundation of all cognition. The verbs in the cycle are: `perceive`, `evaluate`, and `move`. The implicit noun is `existence`.

The *thing* perceived **exists**, the *perception* is **evaluated**, and that evaluation is transformed into a (possibly null) **move- ment**. This means that the fundamental L0 **sentence** is:

perception evaluates to a movement solution

Thus, the meta-language of awareness posits the existence both of the perceived other and a movement solution for it, and assumes — but at the lower levels does not name — the existence of the self doing the perception. The verbs are abstract specifications of functions that are implemented differently in different physical manifestations of cognitively-enabled beings.

Fundamental Cognitive Function

The fundamental cognitive function is $\texttt{compare}(a_i, b_i)$. It is the core operation that makes *knowing* possible. External sensory impressions are reduced by L0 to the **mentacule** data structure[2] which it evaluates by comparing it to inherited archetypes. The **compare** function is implemented anew on each level of the evolved mind to deal with the new objects native to each.

---

[2]Essentially, an array of evacules, or an array of arrays.

Each layer of the evolutionary model contributes to the total information processing abilities that enable us to develop and understand what we recognize as verbal language. Each layer has its own grammar and lexicon — its own language — based on its inherited structures, and implements, or re-implements, the functions needed to process the information in those structures.

L0 Language Elements

The `evacule` is the fundamental structure of L0, and therefore provides its core, concise vocabulary: `hate,love, indifference`.

The L0 action lexicon includes fundamental notions of movement direction that correlate with the archetypal value states of the [a,p,n] evacule:

anti-self/hate : retreat, avoid, maintain

  pro-self/love : approach

  non-self/meh : continue

These are shown graphically in figure 15.1.

Actions associated with these directions are:

    retreat: vigilantly observe - flee - defend

      avoid: carefully observe - maintain

     oblique: casually observe - maintain

    approach: go - attack - pursue - take - consume

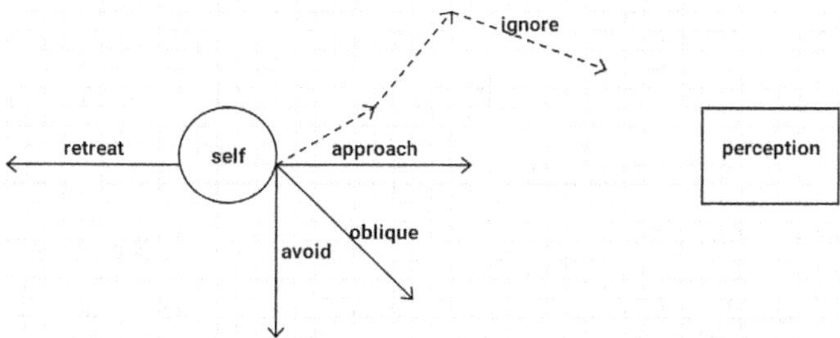

Figure 15.1: L0 spatial perceptual framework

continue: ignore - proceed - seek

Action intensity is related to perception intensity: the greater the threat, the more vigorous the reaction; the more important the opportunity, the more enthusiastic the response. The nature of adjectives and adverbs is that they are defined by the magnitude of the attribute values in the **mentacule**, a structured collection of **evacules**, the evaluation atom. Attribute magnitude (adjective) on the perception side of the sentence is transformed through further assessment into movement intensity (adverb) on the action side of the construct.

The intensity or importance of the perception is expressed in **adjectives** that modify perceived level of the threat or opportunity by adjusting the [a,p,n] parameters of the evacule up or down. In the process of generating an action command, these assigned entity properties are transformed into **adverbs** that modify the specified level of action response.

The equation is simple: if the thing is max *this*, then, unless inhibited by internal status factors, the action will be max *that*. The intensity of the evaluation of the thing's attributes combines with internal state to map to the intensity of the corresponding reaction. The complexity comes from the process that evaluates the many sub-collections of dozens or thousands of evacules in the mentacule's internal and external evacules down to a single actionable evacule value.

The L0 cognitive world can be described by the vector

$$[p, x, y, z, t, m]$$

because L0 sees the world in terms of perceptions, p, in space x, y, z, at time t, that are addressed by movement m. L0 takes in the first five elements and, through the evaluation process, outputs the movement dimension. The t factor manifests only by the comparison of successive perceptions of a given p within a brief period, t, that the brain uses to calculate whether the phenomenon is approaching, receding, or moving obliquely.

In grammatical terms, the basic L0 sentence form is:

```
noun [adjective*] ⟼ verb [adverb*]
```

The **verb** is a reaction to the evaluated input, the **noun**, and there are zero to many adjectives and adverbs.

To illustrate this, an example sentence for a chipmunk might be:

"Approaching **hawk, run** fast!"

The perception→ evaluation→ action cycle is the underlying mechanism that produces the archetypal L0 sentence that identifies the evaluated perception and the calculated response. Note that this is not a *subject - predicate* structure, but a *per-ception - movement* structure, because "hawk, run!" actually represents "(I see) a hawk. Run!"

The first clause of an L0 sentence has a (possibly) modified noun acting as the object of an implicit perception: "[I smell] a **rat**", with only an implied first person subject (since L0 does not support conscious self-awareness). The second part of the sentence is an imperative clause addressed to the first person, rather than the usual second, and is constructed from the evaluation of external and internal sensory input.

The characteristic L0 natural language sentence is:

that [good, bad, indifferent] **thing** is a [threat, opportunity, nothing] **now**, so I will [**seek, avoid, ignore**] it.

The natural language equivalents of the basic L0 sentence are shown in table 15.1.

English sentence	L0 reduction
IDENTIFIER *a* is *b*	Sentences with the verb *to be* assign properties of the known to the new or the unknown. **a** is **b** translates to: perceive **a**, evaluate it to have **b**'s properties, then calculate action from **b**'s properties and the current state of the internal senses.
EVALUATION *a* has qualities *(n..p)* Hate, fear *this*. Love, want *that*. Believe *x*.	Sentences that define a thing's value attributes, however arrived at, are L0 interest-based evaluations. When initiated by higher level reasoning, it is replaced by the L0 value judgment. A belief is an actionable, intense evaluation that corresponds to an inherited archetype.
ACTION do action *a* thus	Part of an L0 sentence if it also contains an `identifier` or an `evaluation` clause.

Table 15.1: L0 characteristic sentences.

L1 Language Elements

The fundamental vocabulary of L1 is: `remember`(store, recall), `recognize`, and `experience`. This core vocabulary supports the L1 ability to *learn from experience*. `Experience` is the locus of value authority in L1, the L1 version of the L0 evacule archetypes that connect all of L0's judgments to the truth as proven by natural selection.

The fundamental L1 functions are: `memorize`, `recall`, `com-pare`, and `recognize`. Experiences are remembered; perceptions are compared with memories and recognized; actions known to be successful are triggered.

Since the dimension of experience is an integral part of everything that the L1 intellect perceives and experiences, the L1 world has more dimensions than the L0 world, and is larger than it because of this. Whereas the L0 world is defined by *stimulus/response* events, the L1 world has the additional dimension of *familiarity*. It's not just that some things are remembered and recognized, it's that *all* things are automatically queried for familiarity and compared for similarity.

The characteristic natural language L1 sentence is:

> **experience/authority** tells me that it is best

> **to do** x in this situation.

Any natural language expression, however complex, that invokes authority, either of experience or of a higher status being,[3] in order to choose an action in the present, reduces to the characteristic L1 sentence. Appeal to authority does not involve higher level reasoning, it defers individual judgment to group power.

L2 Language Elements

As explained previously, L2 is a very large, very complex layer of the mind that might be better divided into three or

---

[3]Personal or institutional authority is a mechanism that validates decisions based entirely on the centrality of the authority in a relevant or important group.

four individual layers, each dedicated to one of the major L2 functions. However, as explained previously, dealing with L2 as a single layer suits the needs of my work, so here we are. However, encompassing distinct, important functions into a single model layer does complicate exposition, so in this presentation, we will divide it into three sublayers that all use the same underlying pattern object: Path, Grouping, and Language.

The L2 level of our intellect is pattern-based, i.e., L2 sees the world in terms of predictable associations of predecessor and successor, or coincident, phenomena, which it stores and recalls in **pattern** objects. Patterns are a linking and nesting organization of data that connect without limit to any number of other connected patterns. Patterns retained in a given $\mathbb{CS}^4$ always form a confluence of connected patterns within patterns, connected to each other by local systems of rules that we call grammar or logic. L2 organizes knowledge into pattern structures because its characteristic inherited structure is the **pattern** object that evolved over time to support the path, word, and rule-based reasoning that allows us to remember and respond to any number of contingencies, and to anticipate a wide array of potential future events.

---

[4]**Cognitive space**, $\mathbb{CS}$, is the formal term for our internal, value laden view of our experience.

Since the purblind defect prevents us from discriminating between L2 and the distinct reasoning processes performed by L0 and L1, people normally conflate them all with L2 functions into a mudball mess that they mistake for reasoning.

L2 Path

`Path` is the lower, pre-verbal area of L2 that enables creatures to memorize and repeat a sequence of steps to complete a task. `Path` supports primitive contingent branching from one pattern object to any of the alternative patterns in the high fan-out exit side of the object.

The fundamental vocabulary of `Path` is: `compare, choose, connect, plan, path, step`. `Steps` are `connected` to form contingent `paths` that can be part of a `plan`, and we choose among alternatives by `comparing` current input with retained knowledge.

L2 Semantic Reality Grouping

Pre-verbal messages, in the form of gestures, expressions, sounds, smells and actions, can communicate information and serve to form/maintain/disrupt social bonds that define groups. From the ℂ𝕊 point of view, one bonds with a group to extend the self beyond the body's boundaries, thus incorporating others into one's own self-interest and power calculation. The essence of grouping is the identification of other with self, and the coordination of individual efforts with those of the group. The fundamental vocabulary of **grouping** is: `agree, join, include`.

L2 Language

The `container` object, an empty pattern object that simply organizes other patterns, is an essential fixture that gives the **Language** level the power to achieve self-awareness. In this essay, we are restricting our focus mostly to pre-verbal language, but the spoken word is a simple extension of the core mechanisms being discussed here. The fundamental vocabulary of the L2 **Language** level is: `validate, reconcile, communicate, abstraction, conditional, type`, and `category`.

Language is the higher, verbal area of L2 that extends the path function to support the complex tree structures that make grammar and language possible. Abstract reasoning is possible in the **Language** region because the type of abstraction we generally use is naturally supported by native L2 structures.[5]

---

[5]In other words, our idea of *abstraction* is an extrapolation of language and classification. This is entirely different than the independent abstractions one finds in formal languages.

The spoken word is just a grammatical branched path of sound groups socially correlated with denotations and shared references that ties the time frames of the three temporal cognitive levels (present, past, future) together into one muddled, but unified, reference frame. The essential concepts of language are a conglomeration of the concerns of the cognitive levels combined with social sharing and obligations.

The language elements discussed so far are a product of the inherited structure and function of the various levels of the cognitive apparatus, so perforce they precede any and all verbal linguistic equipment and ability. The essential vocabulary of language is provided by the structures and supporting functions that naturally arise as the cognitive capability slowly evolves atop an organic substrate. Language initially expresses thoughts and feelings that come from structure, i.e., pre-verbal language articulates existing ideas and internal realities, it does not start from a blank slate, it does not initiate new ideas.

In L2, grammar is the set of rules we define ourselves, or accept from some sub-$\mathbb{SR}$, that govern which patterns in a lexicon can properly connect to other patterns in it. We are generally inclined to see the world in grammatical terms because it satisfies our dual proclivities to see life as conforming to the L2 pattern idiom (even when the patterns are contrived post hoc) and to see life as being governed by rules that center us. The concept of connecting *ideas* together is peculiar to L2, as is the notion that some connections are valid, while others are invalid. The whole notion of sense, of rhyme and reason, of one thing leading to another, is an artifact of the L2 pattern object that underlies all of our higher level thought. But, this is not the only way to see the world, it just naturally arises from the fact that L2 uses a single-entry, high fan-out object to express and organize our abstract thoughts.[6]

Language sentences are used to formulate plans, to create and interpret messages, and to strengthen, maintain, or weaken social links in $\mathbb{SR}$, and to formulate patterns to account for experience. Words are linked to make statements, statements are linked to make patterns that can filter and reconcile input with our sense of order, and input is processed through patterns to anticipate the future so that we might react prior to expected or possible future events.

Validation, in L2 terms, is the process of discriminating between valid and invalid pattern combinations based on internal, self-defined rules. It usually correlates with

---

[6]Defining from-scratch alternatives would be a good thesis topic.

maintaining viable relations with various social groups, but, since L2 is physically isolated from external reality, informal validation *substitutes for* — rather than represents — the discipline of external reality.

The `opinion` object is a specialized form of the `pattern` object that functions to manage message traffic in a such a way as to maintain SR links and CS equilibrium. Rarely, a disruptive message will align with relationship stresses to motivate a realignment of social relations and attitudes for an individual, effectively knocking them out of the orbit of one sub-SR into that of another group, but normally, opinions manage incoming messages in such a way as to maintain current opinions and group affiliations regardless of the unsupportive or contradictory input.

While `value` is a pre-linguistic, interest-based property, `mean-ing` is rooted in an SR language. Sophisticated language can only mature in a robust SR context since it depends on a socially shared lexicon and grammar.

L2 sees the world as a tapestry of patterns, and language is just a collection of phoneme patterns related to each other by a fluid, semi-formal grammar. Since L2 Language conceptualizes ideas exclusively in language, it imagines that ideas actually arise from language, but nothing could be further from the truth. While there are words for all of our thoughts, and most of our feelings, they are applied as labels to pre-existing ideas, they do not create the majority of ideas that are experience and sensation-based.

Verbal language is a pastiche of the pre-verbal language elements from L0 to the L2 Grouping levels. This is to say that, even without the verbal component, even if you did not think the thoughts and say the words, the bulk of your behavior would happen more or less the same, anyway, because the pre-verbal cognitive systems are, unbeknownst to you, still perceiving, evaluating, and generating movement commands whether or not the L2 Language level is participating.

We like to think that most of what we say is rational and reality-oriented, but, in fact, almost none of it actually is, because a *huge* percentage of what we think and say comes, not from our higher cognitive abilities as we suppose, but from the unmediated function of our older, inherited genetic structures and related functions. Even in those cases where abstract thought created by higher reasoning processes does drive our actions, it does so by being translated from the boundlessly complex world of abstraction down into the relatively simple world of action as delineated by the UCM vocabulary shown in table

15.2.

Once the higher L2 Language level evolves the means to conceptualize abstractions, its inevitable first take on consciousness is that there is one and only one mind in us that navigates a sea of troubles and opportunities, driven by unseen, but strongly felt, urges and needs. An immediate consequence of the purblind defect is that L2 will ineluctably misconceive the evolutionary nature of the mind since: a) L2 is convinced that reality can be entirely comprehended with patterns, b) the mind cannot perceive its constituent parts (the defect), and c) understanding evolution requires more layers of abstraction than an individual can conceptualize entirely on his own. Consequently, L2 is linguistically biased towards gravely misunderstanding how our cognitive apparatus actually works, and therefore misleads us into assuming that all problem spaces are adequately described by the contingent branching structure of the pattern object.

The previously discussed language elements inescapably embed our systems of value and meaning into the words and statements of our thoughts, thus endowing our words and sentences with meaning and value. We *know* the functionality of L0-L2 by virtue of being driven by their needs and dictates, and from this our words absorb meaning

L0 - L2 **UCM** Vocabulary	
Cognitive Function	
`compare(`o_1`,`o_2`)`	compare two cognition objects (implemented by each cognitive level for its own object)
Perception-Action Cycle	
`scan`	senses open to continuous input
`perceive`	periodic snapshot of external and internal internal senses
`evaluate`	populate mentacule, evaluate to actionable evacule
`move`	create action command, send to body
`seek`	move perceptual faculty to scan new area
L0	
`hate, love, meh`	the 3 values of the evacule
`true, false, meh`	alternate view of the 3 evacule values
`purpose`	implied purpose: preservation of the good (the self)
`believe`	**belief** is the connection to high [a,p,n] truth
`retreat`	retreat from overpowering threats
`avoid`	maintain distance from manageable threats
`approach`	approach opportunities
`continue`	continue as before when no new threat or opportunity
`thing`	object of perception
`location`	location of thing relative to self
`time`	period between successive, related perceptions
`is`	the 'a is b' metaphor frames L0 knowledge
`do`	'when **A** *do* **B**' action command
L1	
`remember`	both the storage and retrieval of experience lessons
`recognize`	match an input to a memory
`experience`	the stored lesson of a meaningful result
`authority`	truth power delegated to an experience or person
L2 Path	
`step`	a single action
`path`	a sequential series of steps
`plan`	a coordinated set of paths to achieve a goal
`connect`	the ability to chain ideas, steps, or paths together
`choose`	the ability to choose a path in a plan based on an evaluation of circumstances
L2 Grouping	
`join`	extend the definition of **self** to include a group
`include`	attach **other** to **self** for interest calculations
`agree`	transactional assent to join or include **other** and **self**
`rhetoric`	language meant to persuade interested parties to join a group
L2 Language	
`abstraction`	denoting a part as indicative of the whole or a type
`category`	arrange phenomenon by type
`communicate`	message transfer in an $\mathbb{SR}$ vernacular
`reconcile`	process and categorize a message non-disruptively
`validate`	accept a linkage as consistent with a grammar
`logic`	aver statement (in)consistency with a subset of rules
`loop back`	tautology that quells apprehension

Table 15.2: Universal Cognition Model Vocabulary

through their structural roots. We use language to express value and meaning that exists independent of words, we do not learn them through the acquisition of words.

A significant amount of L2 Language function, such as loop backs, is structural, not reasoning, based, because most of our familiar concepts, terms, and actions are fully defined and operational *before* words and verbal ideas are introduced. This entire vocabulary and grammatical structure exists independent of what we think of as rational, or conscious, thought. Most L2 Language capability is part of the universal cognition model and *must* exist in all organic cognitive entities on a given level and below. What this means in a practical sense is that wherever these elements appear in a dialog, they are there not because of anything related to the vaunted 'higher reasoning power' we take so much pride in, but because of primordial instincts and abilities.

The objection that a great deal of thought went into processing higher level ideas before they were reduced to actions based on terms in table 15.2 is unconvincing. To understand why, imagine that you write out your most sophisticated moral or political ideology in a continuous string of words in binary form. Now, imagine summing up the number of bits to get tens, hundreds, or thousands of kilobits. Once you have this in hand, now start randomly flipping bits. Finally, stop and ask yourself, how many bits would you have to flip before your ideology or opinion web became falsified? Certainly, many more than one, or even more than a few thousands. Why is this so? Because the truth of the whole is calculated through a lossy reduction process from the composite pattern complex down to collections of evaluations and evacules that drives to a predetermined conclusion dictated by group norms, not by the content of the data.

The fact is that L2 answers are reduced and written in L0-L2 Grouping terms, which predate the L2 Language you are trying to use to justify conclusions that are almost wholly predetermined by brain structures, some of whose workings we may experience as fate, nature, or a higher power. The question in analyzing a complex situation is not so much "How do I craft a complex, conditional, and flexible response to the situation," but "How do I get from the complex down into the simple UCM actionable vocabulary?" The complex is not carried down into the actionable vocabulary, but is shed as rapidly as possible in order to match the answer predefined in the simple structural L2 grouping language that is maintaining one's bond to a particular group.

L2 Language words can be very complex and abstract, but they must be translated into UCM terms to become actionable. The significance of the analysis shown in table 15.2 is that it locates the elements of language in the various layers of the intellect so that we can understand which of the words we read or hear come from which evolutionary level of the intellect. This allows us to parse the paragraphs and sentences of a source and assign the various clauses to the various intellects, so that we can see that, rather than the whole being a product of reasoning or logic, most of it is pre-verbal in origin, meaning that we would experience these thoughts even without the words, or that the words act as mere triggers to stimulate the primordial thoughts and feelings, rather than the thoughts and feelings being rational responses to a dispassionate review of the evidence.

The thesis behind table 15.2 is that higher level problems can only be solved with higher level reasoning, but anytime any of the terms in the left column of the table occur in a problem-solving exercise it means that an intellect below L3, the locus of higher level reasoning, is controlling the discussion. It is impossible to make progress towards a solution of a higher level problem when this situation obtains. If you tell me you are going to use your reasoning to solve a higher level problem and then tell me you don't even know what an irregular problem space is, or even worse, that you are going to be using your lower level intellects to solve the problem, then I know with absolute certainty that your chance of success is exactly zero, regardless of your political, ideological, or philosophical bent.

Higher level problems exist in irregular problem spaces so, by definition, they cannot be solved by regular problem space solutions devised by lower level reasoning. The reason that your attempt at higher level reasoning cannot solve higher level problems is because only the tiniest fraction of your reasoning doesn't come directly from table 15.2, so the vast bulk of your reasoning is what we might properly call autonomic reasoning that occurs automatically in the lower, more primitive levels of the intellect, and is not high level at all.

The power of table 15.2 is that it succinctly shows how to identify which ideas in your philosophy are lower level, inward facing ideas that spring from organic, evolutionary structures rather than being products of higher level, outward facing L3 reasoning. To make this point clearer to the reader, we will step through the table line by line and explain how the appearance of any of these words or concepts in a dialogue absolutely ensures that the debate is about something other than higher level concepts and problems, and instead is limited to focusing on self-interest, internal feelings, or social grouping concerns.

COMPARE

`Compare` is included in the preamble to the table mostly to clarify for the uninitiated that this one function performs almost all of our reasoning work for us. The `compare` function is reimplemented by each level of the mind for the object it works on: evacules, mentacules, situations, results, patterns, and queries.

Outside of formal languages, it turns out that reasoning is really not that complicated. The ability to calculate angles between vectors has been built into our cognitive hardware since fairly early in the evolutionary process: watch a fetching dog when you throw a Frisbee or a tennis ball: it takes two imperceptibly separate snapshots to gauge the velocity of the throw and observes the angle and direction of launch to fairly instantly calculate in which direction, and how fast it must run to successfully catch the object. The fact that dogs can be tricked to start to run after an object that was never actually thrown, simply confirms that they are calculating direction and velocity based on arm movement before the ball leaves the hand.

Subsequent observations of the ball flight enables them to execute course and speed corrections while running. Baseball players can also do this from a very young age, and neither of these athletes learned the calculation in a math class.

The appearance of higher level reasoning is achieved when the comparison function is used to select between the several exit alternatives in the pattern object, but the mechanism is merely an elaboration of the L0 anti-self, pro-self, non-self calculations.

Perception-Action Cycle Vocabulary

SCAN

Scan is the first command in the Perception-Action cycle. We scan our immediate environment for threats or opportunities of interest, periodically stopping momentarily to take a snapshot of the current state of the senses, which we analyze for significance. Once that perception is processed, the **scan** action continues to examine the field of perceptual focus to look for more threats or opportunities. Scanning is the earliest evolutionary behavior of cognitively capable mobile creatures. Even though, with our advanced mind, we may be scanning for symbolic or semiotic input, the `scan` action, itself, is behavior shared with virtually all volitionally mobile creatures.

PERCEIVE

`Perceive` is used here in the sense of unconsciously taking a snapshot of the current sensory state — including the internal senses — in order to populate the input mentacule with data that will be processed by L0.

EVALUATE

Perceptions are processed by being `evaluated` for anti-self, pro-self, and non-self implications in each of the dimensions of the mentacule (there are potentially thousands of evacules in a single mentacule). The output of `evaluation` is an actionable evacule that can be processed into an action by the Action Module.

MOVE

The action module just creates a `move` command, it does not actually trigger the movement itself, but only transmits the command to the body to execute. The Action Module apparently predates all the variation in the animal kingdom, and has been little changed over the eons of evolution beyond some minor enhancements here and there. The point is that the module produces the `go` command in fish the same as it does in birds or rodents; the different body structures implement the command in their own particular vernacular.

SEEK

The perception-action cycle starts anew when the perceptual field has been exhausted of interest by one or more **scans**, at which time, the organism moves itself to **seek** a new perceptual field to examine. Merely observing critters and wildlife enables one to see that **seek** is actually the default waking action: if there is nothing interesting here, move to seek it elsewhere. We sometimes mistakenly attribute our **seeking** instinct to either curiosity or ambition, but it is only in a state of security or affluence that we come to regard repose as the default state,[7] and **seeking** as the less desirable active state forced on us by deprivation of one kind or another, while it's really the default state of all active beings.

Protolanguage Barriers To Reasoning

The pre-verbal languages native to the various levels of the intellect constitute a protolanguage, a primitive, unspoken language that is the ancestor to our familiar natural lan-

---

[7]Evolution equipped us to struggle, it has not had time to prepare us to luxuriate in a wholesome or productive manner.

guages. Each of these languages are internally focused and self-interest based, while the larger problems we want to solve all exist in external realities. This creates a problem because an inward-facing language is ill suited to tackling problems in external reality. To put it simply, our protolanguage is only capable of expressing ideas about what externalities mean to us, and has virtually no capacity to support extended inquiry into the inner details of independent actors and realities.

In this section, we will go through the vocabularies of the various levels and point out how their use is destructive to higher level reasoning. I am trusting the reader to acknowledge that we, as a species, haven't yet been able to solve any of the larger, non-technical problems. I am also asking the reader to accept the possibility that this is because we haven't developed far enough to enter L3, the domain of higher level, model-oriented reasoning, in significant numbers yet.

The thesis of this section is that the scientific revolution failed to breach the walls of the subjective universe due to the fact that nearly all of our reasoning faculties are inward-facing elements of the protolanguage, which means that they have almost no capacity for exploration and discovery. What we have accomplished has been led by the discoveries of a relatively small number of geniuses that were shared with others through the pattern manipulation facilities of L2. While we have accomplished great things in science and technology, all we have really done is learned how to solve problems in regular problem spaces, which few even suspect are but small subsets of the greater universe of irregular problem spaces.

L0 Vocabulary

The entire L0 vocabulary is built around the tripolar values of the evacule. After reviewing these fundamental values of life, we will look at the interest-based terms in the L0 lexicon.

LOVE, HATE, MEH

The specific L0 vocabulary begins with the evacule terms `anti- self`, `pro-self`, and `non-self`. There are many ways to express this triad of interest, with `love`, `hate`, `meh` (meh = *don't care*) being the emotional version. `True`, `false`, and `meh` are the judgment version we use to express our opinion of the extent to which internal ideas accurately represent external reality. The mechanisms for all of the following terms are exactly the same: `love`, `hate`, `meh`; `true`, `false`, `meh`; `good`, `bad`, `indifferent`, `beau`-

`tiful`, `ugly`, `meh`, etc. All of these terms indicate our personal evaluation of something from our own self-interested perspective. They are not only *not* indicative of higher level thought, they are inimical to it.

Whenever we express a strong attraction or antipathy for anything from plan to idea to person to place, we are thinking with the part of the mind whose only job is to evaluate input in order to be able to decide whether to retreat from, approach, or ignore a perceived phenomenon. This evaluation is not part of the higher reasoning process, it is part of the most primitive calculation of our mortality interests. When tripolar evaluation appears in a reasoning exercise, it forces the discussion to occur at the L0 level, although it may be disguised in higher level terms.

PURPOSE

In addition to higher level concepts of **purpose** that we can craft for ourself, there is a structural bias built into the elemental processes of life that posit that the preservation of the specific, extended, or greater self (the species) is both the immediate and ultimate purpose of life. Purpose is an existential value of the life process, it is a matter of structure, fact, and faith, not of reason (unless we take the trouble to define a transcendent version of it).

Belief

`Belief` is the emotional attachment we feel to archetypal truths or to any ideas or feelings to which we assign an ultimate value. `Beliefs` are `true` in exactly the same way that `true` is `true`. When the discussion topic veers into the domain of `belief`, our focus is on primordial concerns, not higher level reasoning.

Retreat

What is the higher level reasoning form of `retreat`? It doesn't exist, it doesn't need to, because retreat is handled best by the intellect that invented it, L0, and it has no place in a query language. Throughout this discussion, we are identifying actions or ideas that act as markers to place a conversation at a lower level than is adequate for handling higher level problems. But this doesn't mean that these actions are inferior, merely that they cannot contribute to, or participate in, a higher level reasoning process.

`Retreat` is a critically important skill that is best handled by L0, if only because L0 reacts so much faster than any of the higher level intellects. One of the errors historically committed by intellectuals is to deprecate the functions performed by the lower level intellects in favor of slower, less reliable, higher level versions implemented deliberately by supposedly superior intellects. This is an arrogant, frivolous — and, dare I say, *super stupid* — mistake.

Avoid

`Avoid` is one step short of `retreat`, it can be observed in flat lands where prey animals can see predators at a safe distance. The prey will often normally go about their business as long as neither they nor the predator begin to close the gap between them. `Avoidance` is completely inconsistent with the both the spirit and the method of higher level problem solving.

Approach

`Approach` is an activity that brings one closer to a subject with which one wants to engage. It is a valuable action in the L0 sphere, but generally out of place in higher level discussions, where engagement is normally immediate and unreserved. If *approach* comes up in a higher level reasoning exercise, it is generally because *avoid* has already been operative.

Continue

`Continue` is a critical L0 activity that is triggered when ongoing activities are interrupted for an automatic `scan` that confirms no new source of threat or opportunity has entered the perceptual radius. `Continue` simply means what it says, but it is important because it indicates the capacity to temporarily hold an activity in abeyance while scanning for threats, and then resuming the activity at the point of interruption. `Continue` is not inconsistent with higher level reasoning, but it doesn't mean much unless higher level reasoning processes have already been productively engaged and interrupted.

THING

The act of perception makes the `mentacule` representation of a `thing` real enough to be evaluated, whether or not it verifiably exists in any external reality. The overblown philosophical ramblings about the reality of existence are an obtuse consequence of mistaking the perception for the external referent. Thankfully, we are beyond making this kind of mistake anymore since we now know that `we think inside of our head`, and know that the representation *is* the `thing` on which we think, and know that we can only be sure of the relation between it and external reality by going to the effort required to externalize our internal ideas so that they can be verified by independent researchers.

Location

In L0, `location` is defined in terms of self, not in terms of an external grid system. The `location` of other can be described by a qualitative measure of propinquity to self, such as: here, near, or far, etc. At the L0 level, we are always at the origin point when discussing `location`. The reason that `location` without an explicit set of co-ordinates is inconsistent with higher level problem solving exercises is precisely because of the implicit bias of self-interest it represents.

Time

In L0, the concept of `time` is defined as the minimum interval between successive perceptions that can yield sufficient information to determine any change in `location` of a `thing`. In general, as with anything else, if `time` is formally defined it can appear in a higher level problem solving exercise, but if it is qualitative ("urgent", "immediate", etc.), then the discussion has devolved into an L0 discussion of mortality interests.

Is

The verb `to be`, when used to construct a metaphor like *a* is *b*, generally means that *a* is, **in part**, like *b*. This is an L0 reduction of perception to type, and does not appear in higher level problem solving discussions. As always, when used in the formal sense of $a \in \mathbf{B}$, then the use of *is* is just an artifact of the natural language representation of a formal concept. Otherwise, when `is` is used to represent type, quality, or subset of attributes, it is being used in an L0 reduction of input to evaluation, and this cannot occur in a higher level discussion.

Do

The concept of action, of `doing`, is explicitly part of the percep-tion-action cycle, and not part of an advanced problem solving effort in an irregular problem space. Advanced problem solving sessions output models that can be used in the optimization formula to alter the distribution of costs and benefits in a resource allocation problem, but they do not specify a *correct* (i.e., `true`) action. Advanced reasoning outputs a range of possible actions that produce a range of results at a range of costs, it does not output one correct answer, it does not decide between alternatives. At the end of a higher level reasoning exercise, if a mature solution has been defined, then it may be time to decide and do, but this is only after the working session is ready to end.

Interlude

You are undoubtedly saying to yourself, "But, I hear these words in problem solving conversations all the time," and you are right. But problem-solving in the **known** is a normal L2 exercise, while problem-solving in the **unknown** is the advanced L3 activity whose near total absence in human reasoning is what we are trying to account for.

The point is that if the conversation is about decision making, it is L0; if it is based on experience, it is L1; if it is based on trade craft, vernacular, or technical jargon, it is L2. L0-L2 are necessary and valid types of conversations for making decisions and working in the now or in a plan. They are not competent to be involved in problem solving in the unknown, the domain in which we must work if we want to solve complex, human problems we have never solved before.

L1 Vocabulary

Remember

Remember comprises both the storage and retrieval functions of memory. Both L1 and L2 implement the memory function for their native result and pattern objects, but neither L3 nor L0 appear to have much, if any, memory function. Since higher level reasoning is an L3 function, then whenever memory is relied on (except to load resources into $\mathbb{U}$)[8], then the conversation has transitioned from a higher level to a lower level that is governed by authority (L1) or informal logic (L2). Memory can set the table for higher level reasoning, but it cannot otherwise contribute without altering the nature of the interaction.

RECOGNIZE

Recognition is a memory function, and therefore, an L1 and L2 function. **Recognize** is, of course, the whole point of memory, in that it allows you to benefit from experience, to get better at living the longer you live, instead of just older and weaker. During the discovery learning process that is used in higher level reasoning, it is normal to have insights that connect existing patterns together in a novel way, but this is discovery and invention, not recognition. Recognition is followed by implementation of previously learned actions, while discovery is followed by continued exploration from the new waypoint just achieved.

EXPERIENCE

Experience is the stored lesson of a meaningful result, whether good or bad. Experience is a valid and valuable

---

[8]See *General Problem Theory.*

life tool, but it has almost no place in higher level reasoning because some of the greatest discoveries are found when we disregard the lessons of experience to reexamine our most familiar knowledge with a new eye that builds on recently discovered perspectives on both new and old information. While experience may be helpful in defining the boundaries of exploration, in every case we must be willing or even inclined to look beyond that experience in the search for new ways to go forward. Thus, experience, except in the initial stages of an exploratory exercise, rarely fits into a higher level reasoning session.

AUTHORITY

An **authority** is a proxy for an archetypal truth value source. Whether one defers to the authority of a lesson, a group, or a person, the mechanism is the same for all: x is **true** *and unquestionable* because the **authority** says it is. **Authority** renders one's higher faculties powerless to explore and question the boundaries of knowledge, of the possible. **Authority**, whether explicit or not, sacrifices individual freedom in exchange for the actual or imaginary security of staying within the bounds of experience or group approved limits.

For L1, authority is a handy mechanism to codify experience and to support larger social structures that may, or may not, enhance the individual's security. For the average individual, **authority** emotionally recapitulates the experience of security the child felt within a family, whether caring and capable or otherwise.

Authority encapsulates all of the L1 concepts in one term, and is clearly anathema to higher level learning and inquiry.

All of the L1 vocabulary terms fit together to mark an exit from the exploration process and a return to the familiar.

L2 Path Vocabulary

STEP

A **step** can be as simple as an action command, or something as complex as, "transit from point a to point b," but in the context of L2 Path, it refers to one leg in a **path**, or a related series of individual actions. A number of **steps** or **paths** connected by conditional decision points constitutes a **plan**. Whenever these terms appear in a problem solving session, unless explicitly limited to a plan being used merely to get to the next checkpoint, they terminate advanced problem solving because it is impossible to solve a problem in an irregular problem space with a single plan, since replanning at frequent checkpoints is a necessary part of higher level reasoning.

Connect and **choose** are also part of the L2 path vocabulary, but they have corresponding implementations in L3, so these terms do not necessarily indicate a forced end to a higher level problem solving session. That is, using the L2 variant with the L2 truth function terminates higher level reasoning, while using the L3 variant with the L3 truth function does not.

L2 Grouping Vocabulary

Join, Include, Agree

The use of any of the L2 grouping vocabulary terms (**join**, **include** or **agree**), immediately switches the topic of a work session or discussion from higher level problem solving to grouping or social concerns, because it switches the operative truth function from the L3 **viable** and **productive** criteria, to the $\mathbb{SR}$ truth function that is based entirely on group link strength. Switching truth functions away from the L3 level kills higher level reasoning without exception.

Disagree, of course, is part of the **agree** concept and is similarly fatal to higher level reasoning.

RHETORIC

Rhetoric, the use of persuasive language to sway an audience to one's side, is the primary means used by intellectuals and ideologues, alike, to organize and communicate thought. But the purpose of rhetoric is entirely confined to grouping concerns, and as such, is ill suited to be used in the long form query exercises that characterize higher level reasoning. Rhetoric never advances civilization because it lacks the means to formulate or pursue higher level thought, but is just a tool of the L2 Grouping level used to attract partisans to an immediate $\mathbb{SR}$ cause.

L2 Language Vocabulary

Keep in mind that our current discussion only covers nonverbal language, the goal being to demonstrate how much of the content of our idea verbiage predates what we think of as our conscious ideas and feelings. The L2 Language Vocabulary listed below also applies, at least in part, to some of the behavior of our more intelligent primate, corvid, and canine friends, among others.

ABSTRACTION, CATEGORY, COMMUNICATE

The first three terms in the L2 language vocabulary are also implemented in L3, so using them with the L3 truth function does not harm higher level reasoning, but, of course, switching the truth function to the L2 version does, as always, kill it.

Reconcile, Validate, Logic, Loopback

The last four terms in the L2 language vocabulary all relate to processing ideas and input in a way that is nondisruptive to existing opinion webs and social relations. This, obviously, is antithetical to discovery learning, which is inherently disruptive.

Once one gets over the implicitly teleological belief that the purpose of evolution was to produce the current world in all of its finished state, one can begin to appreciate the sloppy, purposeless, randomness that is at the heart of evolution. In general, mutations happen because they do, and they are passed on if they are beneficial, or at least innocuous. If, at some later time, when a decent percentage of the population shares some specific mutations, and the conditions in the species' ecological niche change sufficiently that the non-mutated population can no longer survive, then the mutated population emerges as an identifiably different variant.

An example of a sloppy, random mutation is the L2 ability to predict the future based on the capacity of the pattern object to organize alternative paths using a comparison of the current situation with a collection of possible future situations. The downside of this approach to anticipating the future is that the query inherently returns many more incorrect than correct prognostications. In order to survive this unending torrent of false and worrying predictions, the mind had to have evolved a way (loopbacks) to ignore and disregard most visions of the future in order to focus in on the one or two most likely.

All animals that protect and rear their young share a mutation that allows them to extend the specific self in order to protect family, or to gain strength through allying with, or joining socially, politically, or physically important groups. As a practical matter, it is normally far more important to maintain these relationships than it is to mine for value in social messaging. The `reconcile` function works to cleanup the noisy input channel by preferring to interpret messages in a way that preserves grouping alliances, regardless of the nature of the message content. This is facilitated by the flexibility of the L2 truth function.

The importance of the `validate` function is best illustrated in its absence. This happens when we are dreaming, because the part of the brain that executes this function goes to sleep even though the basic L2 path functions continue to operate. This is why dreams characteristically start with a pertinent theme, but then veer into utterly ridiculous, and even frankly impossible, connections between unrelated ideas. Were we to make these connections while awake, we would severely damage our survival potential, but they generally don't happen because `validate` prevents it. Unless, of course, we are impaired, because intoxication famously also disables our critical faculties.

`Logic` might be said to be a minor part of `validation`, but it seems mostly to be just another rhetorical weapon, and at any rate, it is extremely remote from rigorous reasoning.

Summary

Most of the words discussed in this chapter are inward-facing, protolanguage terms that focus on our mortality interests. They are not outward-facing terms designed to construct an accurate model of externalities, nor even disinterested terms that can be used in the ego-less space in which exploration and discovery learning occurs.

Most of what we think of as reasoning is actually the product of pre-verbal mental processes that are primitive in the sense that they are inward-focused and shared with numerous other species still alive today. Most of our thinking is not all that far beyond what a squirrel or a dog can do, with the sole exception of self awareness, which can be attributed strictly to the fact that part of our organic inheritance is the `container` object that makes some level of self awareness (self naming, for example) possible.

Neither the language nor the reasoning process known or practiced by ordinary souls or self-styled intellectuals is designed or able to tackle higher level problems in irregular problem spaces.

The reason humans cannot yet begin to solve higher level problems is because very few have found the path into the L3 area in their mind, and even fewer have been motivated to live in it long enough to master the long-form query, the indispensable tool of the exploration and discovery process.

Chapter 16

Next

Where do we go from here? There's a fork in the road that seems to have two branches: we go down one if all we want to do is make our life somewhat better by significantly improving our reasoning, or we can go down the other if we want to explore the powers of the L3 intellect.

The question down the first path is, "Can we use the fascinating ideas presented in this book in our personal and work lives?" This is exactly where we started this book, and the answer is still the same: I'm not the carpenter, you are. You would have to figure out through experimentation how much of this could be leveraged to make your normal reasoning more effective. I suspect that understanding what's really going on behind passionate arguments at home or in the office might put you in a better position to play the long game without getting caught up in L0 belief struggles. I could see that. It's also hard for me to see how understanding realities, truth, opinions, attitudes, and the rest would do anything but help you understand your world better and quicker. But, this really is up to you. If you figure something out, maybe you could write a book about it.

The other branch in the road involves exploring the L3 discovery intellect, a choice that I cannot help but endorse since I've been living it myself for so long. The best way I can see for you to start down this road would be to read all of the relevant material you can get your hands on. The available library is not that large.

The first book to look into is *Super Stupid: Why The Educated Elite Are So Wrong So Often About So Many Things*. After that, you should be ready to tackle the hard stuff:

- *Ultrareasoning: Principles And Practices of Faceted Model-Oriented Reasoning*
- *The Structure Of Truth*
- *General Problem Theory: A Framework For Problem Solving In The Unknown*

You would have to do quite a bit of studying because productive, higher level reasoning requires a prior knowledge of:

- the difference between internal and external knowledge;

- the role of evolution in defining the cognitive process;

- the definitions of science and reality;

- the different truth functions;

- the properties of the unknown;

- how to reliably perform exploration and discovery in the unknown.

You've just been introduced to these concepts. It's a long way from here to mastery. You can go further than you have.

The only remaining barrier stopping us from using the extended scientific method to systematically cultivate objective knowledge in the subjective sphere — just as we do in the objective sphere — is us. Most of us don't realize that we already have the necessary tools at hand to do the job.

Get to work.

Index